THE TUFF LUV GUIDE TO

HAPPINESS

21 SECRETS THEY DIDN'T KNOW TO TELL YOU…AND MORE

MIKE DANN

AKA, WRITER-BOY

www.happiness-quotes.com

Also available on Lulu.com

ISBN 978-0-6152-1591-4

Library of Congress: 2008930318

CONTENTS

PART I. WHAT IS HAPPINESS?

PART II. OBSTACLES TO HAPPINESS

PART III. 21 SECRETS TO HAPPINESS

1. Set HAPPINESS Goals
2. Lower Your Standards
3. Take Care of Your Vehicle
4. Maintain A Positive Outlook
5. Work Out, Eat Right
6. Stop, Drop and Roll
7. It's How Important?
8. Two Words To Set You Free
9. Slow Down
10. Spirituality
11. Be Creative
12. Live for Today, Plan for Tomorrow
13. Do Something for Someone
14. Live Every Day Like It's Your Last
15. Lighten Up
16. Treat Yourself
17. Appreciate What You've Got
18. Get a Life
19. Enjoy
20. Find the Joy
21. Happiness Is A Choice

Foreword

I am the book you are reading and…whoa-- hey, watch the hands, Freshy. That's better. Either you bought me because you want to be happier, or someone gave me to you because you're in some kind of unhappy negative funk and you are in need of something, anything to get you out of it. Well if you are negative, now hear this…negativity, just like happiness, is a choice. It is you and only you who decides how happy you want to be, and this is quite possibly the most important lesson of your life—and the hardest to remember when your situation makes you want to scream "Life sucks."

If you are jaded or cynical, you'll need to dump those. They are nothing more than hard candy shells you put up to protect your soft chocolaty interior from the words and deeds of others that serve to make you feel small, whether they were intended to or not. What can protect you from others if you drop your negative defense shields? Self-esteem, self love. Not conceit, but a personal *knowing* that you are a good, intelligent person, whose positive outlook, confidence and happiness, cannot be swayed by the actions of others—others with self-esteem so low that they try to build themselves up by making you feel small.

By the time you finish reading me, your self confidence will soar, and you'll project a personal image so positive that people will feel better about themselves when they are with you. The outside world will have no negative effect on your happiness because you'll know that happiness is a choice to be made ahead of time, and sustained by a positive outlook, which anyone can acquire.

Now as you read, it is I, the book who will be whispering sweet nothings into your brain, not the guy who wrote me. He was negative too. In fact, he thought I could make him happier, and for once, he was right. And now that he's used me to increase his own HAPPINESS, he wants to truly share the gift of me with you—at the low, low price of (market value here). I can help you, but you have to do your part by desiring to be happier. I'll tell you right now—if you don't want to be happy, you certainly won't be, no matter what I tell you. Hey, quit slouching, duck-breath. No offense to you real ducks.

You have just taken your first test, which we will grade now and correct to 100%. Were you in any way offended by the duck-breath comment? If the answer is no, you pass. You are ready to be happier and more positive than you already are by reading on. If you were offended, however, you're farther gone than I thought—Nurse, get me two twinkies, a flashlight, vise grips, a monkey and a trombone. Quickly now put a twinkie in the patient's mouth to shut them up and protect us from the toxic negativity and self-important seriousness that might spew out and get on our shoes. Now put a twinkie in my mouth because I love them and play happy birthday into the patient's left ear on the trombone…Vise-grips--let's see here—good God the negativity has morphed into a…stick. I can't reach it, it's too far up. Send in the monkey. Wait…abort, abort, get that primate out of there before we lose—that was close. Yeah, hose him down and buy him a steak. We're going to have to do this the hard way—by somehow combining words together whereby the patient will become positive, easy going and happy naturally. I'm going to need another twinkie…

Whew! I hope that wasn't you who failed the test. If it was, sorry, it's an important part of Tuff luv, and the beautiful beginning of a happier you. Now, to reiterate, the sooner you understand that the voice you read is mine (the book) and not the writer's, the better you will understand the points in each chapter. I will be talking about Writer-Boy (the writer) and many of his antics throughout the book as examples of what not to do if you want to be happy. I'll also point out some things about happiness that I've taught him along the way. I will be using many endearing names for him, and I will also be throwing some of that your way too, duck-breath, (just checking) to make sure you're awake and not taking yourself too seriously.

Fasten your seatbelt, for together we are going on a journey to the center of your brain to find out what makes you tick, and when we get there we are going to tweak those gelatinous globs of goo into a happier, less stressed, worry free, self-confident, even-keeled you—without the cynical, jaded, hard candy shell.

In section I, we'll define HAPPINESS, then in section II we'll go into worry and other obstacles to HAPPINESS, then in section III, you'll use the 21 proven secrets to eliminate worry, frustration, anger, anxiety and other dastardly garbage you might allow into your skull that can deny you HAPPINESS. Gang, we're taking out that garbage, starting now.

The purpose of this book is to help you humans attain world peace through personal happiness. There will be peace on Earth one day, with or without you. If you don't figure world peace out soon, in the immortal musical stylings of Capt. Quint of "Jaws"…"Farewell and adieu to you fair Spanish ladies--farewell and adieu to you ladies of Spain. For we've received orders for to sail back to Boston—and we may never see you again". That would be the "without you" version of world peace.

By the way, who are "they" who didn't know the 21 secrets to tell you? They would be whom ever didn't tell you the 21 secrets because they didn't know them to tell you. Parents, teachers, whom ever they are, I am not one of them. You will not be one of them either, because you will know the 21 secrets and can pass them along to those who aren't aware. Twinkie time!

PART I.

WHAT IS HAPPINESS?

For different people HAPPINESS means different things. For some, it might be winning the lottery. For others, it might be losing weight, traveling to exotic destinations, finding the love of their life, or parking their open mouth under the chocolate fountain on the lido deck until it runs dry. Still others might define HAPPINESS as being content and at peace with who and where they are in life. HAPPINESS for all humans is this nothing more than a state of mind. Remember that as you travel through my pages.

It's pretty obvious to me that most of you humans seek HAPPINESS from outside sources, deciding what goal you need to achieve or item you need to acquire for that magical moment of HAPPINESS to occur. But if you should reach that lofty goal or get that magical toy, how long will that HAPPINESS last? Will it be only a moment, or will it linger for days or even months? Let's face it—six months after you buy that car you've always wanted it will just be your car. And people who win the lotto sometimes find out they wish they hadn't. Now you no longer have to wait to be happy, I will help you get happy now. Hey, You better keep reading and don't make me come over there and give you another stickectomy. Oh, that wasn't you? Sorry. Where *is* that monkey anyway?

The problem with your HAPPINESS being dependant on some goal or outside force, is that one, you may never reach that goal, and two, what will your state be in the meantime? If you never reach that goal, will you never be happy? The meantime you spend between your goals is your life. It is this meantime that must be spent at the same level of HAPPINESS as the day you attain one of your worldly goals. If you can achieve such a high state of HAPPINESS while you live every day on the way to your next milestone, you will live a happy life, not merely attain a happy goal whose HAPPINESS fades with time.

What if, even as you pursue your worldly goals, you maintain a daily goal of enjoying each day, each minute for what it is—an opportunity to own and use, any way you want, the most priceless, ever-diminishing commodity known to man. It is so precious that it cannot be bought, horded, or traded, and many of you treat it like so much trash. "Tell me!" screams your brain.

All right. But your reaction to the answer will indicate to you how you treat this gift, this treasure. It is your allotted time on this planet. It is finite. Just as it began, so it will one day end. And every portion of it that you choose to spend on misery, hate, depression, worry, anger, or any other negative emotion defiles it, destroys it, wastes it. This very time you might waste in negativity could be spent in love, joy, HAPPINESS if you choose, but one thing for sure-- once it is gone, it's gone. And the whole of your life, your time here, at its end, will be less than what it could have been for every second you spent in negativity.

Ok kids, here it is, the very definition of happiness according to Forrest Writer-Boy. The first pre-requisite to a happy state is the lack of negative thoughts, feelings, or emotions. You're not sad, angry, frustrated, scared or experiencing any other negative emotion that by default, will bring you down. This is the most basic form of HAPPINESS. Higher HAPPINESS is how you feel when you have met the first hurdle of no negative thoughts feelings, or emotions, AND you are experiencing any of the following thoughts, feelings, or emotions:

GLADNESS, LUCKY, LOVED, APPRECIATED, APPRECIATIVE, GRATITUDE, ANTICIPATION, EXCITEMENT, FUN, LAUGHTER, GIVING, KINDNESS, GOOD HEALTH, COMFORT, WELL-BEING, ACCOMPLISHMENT, JOY, PEACE OF MIND, TAKEN-CARE-OF, INTELLIGENT, FORTUNATE, CONFIDENT, CONTENTED, BELONGING, SELF-SUFFICIENT, MOTIVATED, CAUGHT-UP, ON TIME, CREATIVE, SPONTANEOUS, SAFE, MORAL, LOGICAL, PLEASED, PLEASANTLY SURPRISED, TRUSTWORTHY, LIKED, RESPECTED, GOOD-LOOKING, or any other positives you can think of. To know that these and other positives are contributors to happiness, and to enjoy them as they are happening, is to experience true happiness. Yes, you have experienced and wasted a huge amount of happiness that went unnoticed, unappreciated, and unknowingly ignored.

There are so many ways to feel happy that for those who desire it, a level of happiness is only a conscious realization away. When you feel the thoughts and emotions mentioned earlier, instead of just being a spectator, remember to take control of them, enjoy them, know that right now, you are in a state of happiness, the intensity of which is determined by your level of appreciation, which is determined by your outlook. If your outlook is positive, you will appreciate feelings of happiness with more intensity. If your outlook is negative, we'll fix that, but for now give yourself a ten minute time-out.

Can you control your feelings of appreciation through thought and attitude? Ah, yeah. Can you force yourself to suppress and banish negativity when it rears its ugly head? Uh, yeah. Ok, if the feelings mentioned before are hard to come by for you, they won't be by the time you finish reading me.. But don't worry, after you're done and the negativity is gone, we'll send in the chimp just to make sure.

Just remember--all things can be looked upon in a positive light or a negative light. The light you choose will determine your happiness. Tennis anyone?

YOUR INNATE HAPPINESS

    Your tendency toward HAPPINESS, regardless of outside events or influences, good or bad, is what we will refer to from now on, as your INNATE HAPPINESS. Your INNATE HAPPINESS is mainly influenced by your own subconscious and conscious views of yourself and your world, and the mental "cruise control" that you maintain in the absence of outside influences. It is your neutral point, or the level of HAPPINESS your mind always returns to after the effects of any outside influences have worn off. In other words it is your pre-pondered or predetermined state of happiness that you have chosen for yourself.

    For some, their INNATE HAPPINESS might be very low and for others very high, but only you can make that determination. This predisposition toward HAPPINESS in the absence of outside influence can be assigned a numeric value, and I'll ask you to do that shortly. Keep in mind, you have already chosen your INNATE HAPPINESS.

In order to establish your INNATE HAPPINESS value, we must calibrate the scale on page 14 to your personal definition of true happiness. You'll notice that -10 is the value you'll place on the lowest recollection of your life up to now, and +10 is the value for the happiest recollection of your life up to now. The scale is based on your previous life experience. Hang on to your hats kids, because you are about to find something out about yourselves that not even you knew! What was the happiest time or experience of your life, your personal definition of +10? How did it feel? How long did it last? Does thinking about it now make you feel good? Do it. Go back RIGHT NOW to that place and time and remember it as vividly as possible, for at least 5 minutes. I'll wait…

Well, for whatever time you spent dwelling on your +10, how did you feel? Pretty good eh? So by merely directing your thoughts, you have spent a few happy minutes that might otherwise have been spent, well, not as happy. Now here's the kicker. How do you compare that happiest time of your life, your +10, to the happiest you could possibly ever be? I'm talking about the best thing you could dream of actually happening to you. Is there something, anything that could possibly beat your previous +10? Only you know.

Let's compare your previous +10 to that ultimate happiness defined. If you did finally reach your ultimate, how would you feel compared to your previous +10? Even happier, or about the same? Writer-Boy contends that ultimate HAPPINESS, like your INNATE HAPPINESS is something you decide upon ahead of time. Your previous +10 was, at the time, your ultimate HAPPINESS. What would you do differently as a result of reaching your new ultimate? Cartwheels, back flips, what? Maybe…not. Maybe through your previous +10, your mind has already experienced ultimate happiness, or the happiest you could ever let yourself get, and the feeling may just be the same even if you do reach that new pie in the sky , and that would mean—Yes, you have already experienced ultimate happiness *and you didn't even know it.*

HAPPINESS SCALE

+10 Euphoria, Bliss, Doing Cartwheels

+9

+8

+7

+6

+5 Moderately Happy

+4

+3

+2

+1

  0 Mere Existence

-1

-2

-3

-4

-5 Moderately sad

-6

-7

-8

-9

-10 Desperate, hopeless, eating worms

Alright, back to placing a number value on your personal HAPPINESS. Interpolate the scale on page 14 and find the number you think corresponds to your average, uninfluenced mood. If you think you are a -10, give me your belt, and holy cow—get away from the window. If you think you are a +10 and are completely bubbling over with HAPPINESS, be very careful, as other humans will be incredibly jealous, and may just want to squish your twinkies.

Let's say you decide you are a +4. That will be the baseline from which you will measure changes to your INNATE HAPPINESS itself, as well as how different events affect your current HAPPINESS, or how you actually feel at any given time. Though outside influences may affect your current HAPPINESS temporarily, your INNATE HAPPINESS comes mainly within, not from without. In other words, you have unconsciously already decided on your level of happiness which of course means that you control how happy you want to be.

You can use the same scale to determine your current HAPPINESS, which, at any given time may be higher or lower than your INNATE HAPPINESS, and can be attributed to outside influences to the extent that you let them. If your current HAPPINESS is low, you will use tools described in later chapters to raise it. If your current HAPPINESS is high, you will also be given tools to hang on to and even recreate that desirable state.

Some people don't want to be happy, don't care to be happy, and wouldn't know if two tons of it hit them right in the face. It's amazing, but true. These people dwell on negatives and when something good happens to them it might bring their state up from -5 to -4, or they might even find something bad about it and lose a couple points. Instead of being happy about getting the leaky pipes fixed, they dwell on how they got "screwed" by the plumber or how the world is going down the tubes or the nerve of so-and-so.

Or they can't stop talking about how stupid, bad, ridiculous or strange other people are. If you know someone that gets a +10 out of negativity, don't let them drag you down to their level or I'll send the chimp over to perform a negativectomy.

People who want to be happy find the positive in everything, and dwell on it. They try to see all things and circumstances in a positive light, are pleasant to strangers, and try to live every second to its fullest. They realize that most others don't even know that HAPPINESS is a choice, and try to spread it around when the opportunity arises. No, you don't have to grab a stranger's hand and break into Kumbaya—in fact, don't. But a positive comment, an opened door, or letting another driver merge in front of you are small, positive gestures that, if everyone decided to take part in, could actually increase the collective HAPPINESS.

Try it. Do something for, or say something nice to a stranger occasionally, and expect nothing in return. Your reward may only be the feeling you get when you know you have at least tried to increase the HAPPINESS of the world. But when you do good things for others, the good will come back to you sooner or later. It's the "what goes around comes around" theory. Do good and good will come back to you. Do bad and bad will find you. Smiles everyone!

OUTSIDE INFLUENCES

Your INNATE HAPPINESS is an inside choice you make, and should not be affected by work, the stock market, people, rain or anything else. Because you are human, you allow outside influences to influence your current HAPPINESS, and possibly your INNATE HAPPINESS. If you do allow outside forces to change your INNATE HAPPINESS, you lose! You have allowed circumstances beyond your control to dictate your happiness. Some examples of outside influences that might lower your current HAPPINESS in the short term would be a traffic jam, being late, a speeding ticket or a snide comment from a supervisor or co–worker.

Consciously prevent these events from overshadowing your positive attitude by accepting them, and allowing them to exist because they already do, knowing that negative feelings will not make them go away. As for a verbal assault from someone, it's bigger to ignore a negative comment than it is to make one.

As for positive events, such as getting a raise or noticing a beautiful day, teach yourself to bask in the them, lingering in the good they give off by mentally listing all the good feelings that result from them. When your mind recalls these positives less and less, force yourself to relive the feelings often. The more your mind stays on the positive, the happier you will be.

As for the negative influences, simply allot them as little brain-time as possible and move on. Let's say someone mentioned that you are looking fatter than usual. Again, don't give such a comment the time of day, and forget about it—forever. Don't dredge that mental junk up again because you will feel the same anger, hurt and embarrassment you felt when it happened, and why would you put yourself through that again?

Another example of that kind of outside influence, and one that effects a lot of people, is the possibility of getting "downsized", or being let go by your employer at a point where you've invested too much time in your current company to ever really recover. My creator had (yes, even the Self-proclaimed-Happy-Master has bad day now and then) such a day yesterday.

Someone mentioned to Writer-Boy in passing, the huge amount of money his employer lost last year, and that set the mood for the rest of the day. It got so bad that Bag-Lady-Man envisioned himself in some grey, dark, downtown area pushing around a shopping cart containing all his belongings. He saw himself as a bag-lady, though he knew he would never let it happen. No offense to you real bag ladies.

So last night, Mr. Miserable starts thinking about how I'm (the book you're reading) going to be a success, and comes up with more ideas, including ideas for more books in a possible series. Then he decides that in the morning he would make some calls about other interests. Both calls are a smashing success, he works out, does some household chores and comes up with one of his happiest days in weeks. Yet NOTHING changed related to the possibility he could lose his job for which he has trained for most of his life. He simply thought about other things, because in fact, he had NOT lost his job, and decided NOT to worry about it until it happened, if ever.

If and when he did lose his job, he would not simply worry about it, but the situation would require immediate, effective action, even if that meant working at McDonald's (no offense to you McDonald's workers. As a matter of fact, Writer-Boy worked there during college, and the thought of having to clean a perfectly spotless picture window seemed pointless so he would apply a liberal blob of sputum (that's loogie to me and you) to it, then clean it while enjoying a good laugh).

Why Writer-Boy felt the need to share that tidbit of excess information I don't know, but getting back to getting laid off of his current job…There simply wouldn't be time to worry. The situation, if it came about would require immediate attention. Because it had not happened yet, he decided to recognize the possibility, and forget about it, focusing more on immediate responsibilities and the getting on of living a happy life. Listen to me—You will never worry about a maybe again.

Outside influences, whether good or bad are just that. The positive ones should help maintain your high INNATE HAPPINESS and the negative ones should not affect you at all, except you'll take the things they teach you and use them to your advantage. Hey, now!

INSIDE INFLUENCES

I hate to be the one to break the news to you, but in order to be happy most of the time, you actually have to work at it. HAPPINESS, like a good relationship, is not something that requires no maintenance. It must be constantly fed in order to keep it alive. The food of HAPPINESS is positive thinking. You are not born happy. Consequently, most of you go through life in a basic state of existence, and occasionally have cause to consider yourselves happy for whatever reason.

When you find yourself getting mad at your boss or the increasing cost of living or something you saw on the news, stop and drop the subject from your mind. These are things over which you have no control, and to keep thinking about them only causes stress. Let's get this straight right now. *STRESS AND WORRY ARE HARMFUL TO YOUR HEALTH!*

My goal is to help you maintain a high level of INNATE HAPPINESS that will allow you to get more out of your time on Earth. Every second you spend hating, worrying, stressing, or in a state of uneasiness is a waste of time. If you can't control a situation, forget it. If you can control it, make your plan for how you will change it, and then forget about it until you are ready to take action. Don't fall into the worry trap. Your mind naturally loves to hash things out over and over with no conclusion in sight. It must be recognized as the useless waste of time that it is and stopped immediately.

There are days when you wake up and all the world seems right, yet nothing happened since the day before to create that feeling. What we are trying to do here is create that feeling every day. When you wake up feeling great, try to figure out why, and if you do narrow it down, do that all the time, whatever it was. This isn't brain surgery here, kids, it's just feeling good. It's not hard!

The main determinant of your INNATE HAPPINESS from the inside is your mindset. Are you negative or positive in your everyday views? Positive people are much happier than negative people. Brilliant observation there by HAPPINESS-Man, eh? As simplistic as the statement seems, why doesn't everyone get a positive mental attitude? Because either they don't know how, they don't know that they can, or they just don't want to because they are who they are and by God that's the way it is. Total hard candy shell.

Anyone, no matter how bitter and jaded, can acquire a positive attitude. You have already chosen the status of your attitude, either consciously or by default. If it isn't positive enough right now to make you a happy human, you can choose to change it. No, you don't have to get a whole new head like Frankie, you just need to change the way you perceive things.

Most of you humans react to outside influences, and without those influences, you simply drone through life on autopilot, trying to maintain the mundane comfort of the status quo. When unexpected changes to the status quo arise, you humans concentrate your thought and energy in getting things back to the way they were, and you won't be happy until they are. The problem with that modus operandi is that maybe you weren't all that happy in the first place, and now you have to work harder just to have things as good as they were before the change came about. If you are like this, you are allowing outside influences to determine your INNATE HAPPINESS. Why would you allow circumstances beyond your control to decide how happy you are when you can make the decision yourself? Exactly.

By simply choosing to be happy, all the time, regardless of outside influences, you can overcome all negative events to maintain the high level of HAPPINESS that you choose. Sure, there will be life events that will test your chosen level of HAPPINESS, probably the worst being the loss of a loved one, and mourning such a loss is natural and healthy. But at some point, you pick yourself up and go on living, just as the person you lost would have wanted. No amount of misery or sorrow or guilt will bring them back, and yes, you can be happy after such a loss. Writer-Boy's been there—and you can and will recover. It may take more time for some than others, but HAPPINESS is possible after *any* loss. Appreciate all you have now, for one day you will have to let it all go.

Part of the wonder of you humans is your amazing ability to roll with changes and bounce back from any adversity, often times turning adversity into something positive. Knowing ahead of time how you will react to things that happen in your life will better prepare you for any eventuality.

You humans cannot see into the future, which means that by definition, your futures are uncertain, and therefore unknown. You can anticipate the unknown with excitement or cower before it in fear. Which one do you think a positive person would choose? Which one have you chosen up until now? Which will you choose from now on? Have you noticed that the way you view yourself, your world, your circumstances is a choice made by you, whether consciously or not? Now that you know you can, do. Choose wisely, Grasshopper.

PART II.

OBSTACLES TO HAPPINESS

WORRY

HAPPINESS-Man woke up today feeling well-rested, peaceful, and content. Then a cannon ball slammed into his head and the mood went down from there. The cannon ball was shot into his brain from—you guessed it, his own brain! The cannon ball represented worry over a situation that occurred at work yesterday. He said something innocently to a co-worker that might have been construed as a slur. Had our boy realized his foot-in-mouth, he'd have apologized immediately, but he didn't. Nothing was meant by it but if the co-worker was offended, and complained, there could be trouble.

At the time of the incident, Peter Panic thought nothing of it. But later, when his naturally paranoid brain replayed the day, he became more and more worried that he might have to talk his way out of something while "on the carpet". So he worried all afternoon and into the night, and surprisingly enough, slept well. When Panic Attack woke up, he remembered his possible problem and began to worry for the second day in a row over something that had not happened. He asked me to tell you, by the way, that he's not perfect, and that even if he thinks he knows how to teach HAPPINESS, it doesn't mean he's not susceptible to the same worries you are.

So he wasted several hours worrying, then decided to continue working on me. At the top of the page was typed one word—worry, which is the subject of this chapter. The rest of the page taunted him with it's blank whiteness, almost laughing at his uncanny ability to overlook the obvious. When IQ Of What It Used To Cost For A Gallon Of Gas finally caught on, it was like a revelation. The very problem that plagued his mind with uneasiness for the last day and a half, was the very answer to the problem of what to write in this chapter on worry.

What a serendipitous break. Suddenly, the problem that had Furrowed-Brow mired in counter productive, negative thought had become a *solution*. He decided to recount the original problem, and write it as it happened, allowing both he and you to find out how it would eventually play out together. Would the co-worker turn our boy in? Would all that worry have been for nothing, or would he get a verbal spanking and possible disciplinary action? Without really noticing, Pen Scraper had *stopped worrying* about the problem and became more curious than fearful as to its final resolution.

A great weight had been lifted, and the problem, either way it would turn out, ceased to matter, because *in Writer-Boy's mind,* it was more powerful as a solution than it was as a problem! This lead to another Aha moment for our boy. It would seem then, that all things being equal, a positive thought carries more weight than a negative one. Could a person, worried or sad or mad, run his problem through a positive train of thought and lift the negative stress from his mind? Why not? Let's face it. Writer-Boy's problem had not changed, his thinking changed. He still faced the possibility of having to kiss someone's butt, but his attitude toward it changed, and he simply ceased to worry about it.

What if one took every thought of fear, stress, sadness, worry, hatred, anger, or any other negative emotion that causes your human minds to experience unease and view it through a positive mental attitude? Hey, call it rationalization or whatever you want, but if exhaustive searching for the positive in a negative situation can turn darkness into light, why wouldn't you humans do it every time?

The next time you are faced with a heavily negative thought or problem, ask yourself these questions:

What is good about this?

How can I turn this situation into something positive?

What can I learn from this?

Is it really *that* important?

Obviously, each problem you humans face in life is different, but if you look long enough for a positive solution, and still can't find one, then the very act of thinking positive while searching for a solution is in itself a good and mentally healthy exercise. As I mentioned before and will again, recognize the situation causing you uneasiness, and if possible, take action. If no immediate action is possible, create a plan, then forget about it until you need to take action. Stewing over things that cannot be immediately resolved is a waste of time, especially if you find out later that your concerns were over nothing at all.

Writer-Boy thinks that paradoxically, there is positive energy for all negative energy, which is in step with the scientific theory that the energy of the universe is a constant that only changes form. Thoughts are energy. You can find positive things hidden in all negative situations if you look hard enough. Even if you can't find the positive in a situation, the act of searching will in the end make you a happier person, simply because positive thoughts are positive energy. Here is a real life example of a positive born of a negative:

While in pilot training a budding navy fighter pilot was in a horrible auto accident that required the removal of his spleen accompanied by a long and painful recovery. He eventually won his wings and went on to fly F-8 fighters from aircraft carriers. On a particular mission, while flying low over the ocean, there was an explosion in his fuel system that caused the plane to tumble uncontrollably, and oh yes, catch fire. His ejection seat malfunctioned and he had to jump out, risking hitting the tail as it raced by. He cleared the tail, only to find that when he pulled the D-ring that would deploy his parachute, his tumbling caused the chute lines to tangle around the canopy, rendering it useless.

The pilot hit the ocean at high speed, sustaining major injuries that the flight surgeon told him would have killed him—if his spleen had not been removed years before. Things that initially seem bad have ways of not being that bad later, or are catalysts that cause a person to move in a better direction, or as in the case of the pilot, the auto accident in training allowed him to survive a failed high speed ejection years later. Is there an event that you have gone through that initially seemed like the worst that could possibly happen, only to find out later that it caused another positive event that would not have transpired without the "bad" experience? Think a while.

By the way, HAPPINESS Man's "problem" turned out to be nothing, but just remember that once he turned his problem into a solution, he was happier than if he had never experienced the problem at all. You can do the same with your worries, or use the plan of action method mentioned above, whether your worries are financial, medical, marital, any kind of worry at all. All you have to do is try. "Hey, stop worrying you knucklehead" is what I say to Writer-Boy when he needs it and your orders are to say those beautiful words of wisdom to yourself when you need it. Now drop and give me twenty, marshmallow—no, real ones.

FEAR

There are many things in your world to be afraid of; losing your job, disease, terrorism, and Writer-Boy's all time favorite--spiders. These are but a few that you just have to live with. First we will concentrate on two similar, debilitating fears, either of which could keep you at a lessened INNATE HAPPINESS, yet both of which you can control. Then we will look at other things that make your stomach quiver.

The first two are fear of success and fear of failure, and we'll cover these because they are hard to spot, and can do huge amounts of damage to your HAPPINESS. Fear of failure is not much different than fear of success. Fear of failure is obvious, but how can anyone be afraid of success, you wonder.

Let's say you are trying to quit smoking. You will most likely tell your friends and family about your big goal, because people that are passionate about their goals can't help but talk about them, and you should be passionate about your goals. What? You're not passionate about your goals? You mean you are just "trying to quit smoking"? Or "trying to start a business" or "trying to lose weight"? If you are only "trying", and the goal is difficult, you have not committed yourself to it and most likely, until you have committed yourself to it, you will not attain it.

Why would you say that you are trying to lose weight? Well, in your mind, you feel that the word "trying" is giving you an out just in case it doesn't happen, and so you will (in your own mind) save face when you are eating cake and someone asks about your diet. Next time you want to tell someone you are "trying" to attain some lofty goal, tell them that you really want to make more money or lose weight or whatever, but that you probably won't because you're just not committed. In other words, you wish you could do something, you will take little or no action toward it, and you tell people you are "trying" to do it, knowing full well it isn't going to happen. How do I know this? I just watched Lazy-Man stare at the TV for five hours when he should have been writing me. He tells people he's "writing a book about HAPPINESS", then writes a couple paragraphs and forgets about it for a couple weeks.

As I sit here being written, I wonder if he'll finish me, and if he does, will he stop short of what it takes to cause world peace? If so, it could be fear of success or failure, or better yet, rejection. I don't know and I don't think he does either. For the last twenty-two years, the Master-of-Beginnings has started dozens of projects, only to quit them before they even had a chance. Except for writing. Eleven years ago, Project-Man decided to write an article and sell it to a magazine. They bought it. Then he wrote a few letters to editors, and every one was published. Then he decided to write about a personal adventure, and he sent it to the premiere magazine on the subject, and they bought that one too.

So now Hemingway-Man thinks that he should be able to sell anything he writes, but because he wants to keep his 100% sales record, he quits writing, fearful of rejection or maybe he knows there's only one place to go when you're on top. So he quits writing for several years, then decides to "try" it again. He sends out several half-baked story ideas to magazines, though none of the subjects really interest him, secretly hoping to get rejected so he doesn't have to actually write about something that bores him. The passion of his earlier successes had faded, and he got several rejection letters, much to his relief. He did not believe in his own ideas, and that must have been reflected in his proposals.

He was afraid of success (getting the assignment), and his fears of rejection came true. What am I getting at? If you don't believe in it, neither will anyone else, and it simply won't happen. Before announcing to the planet of your grandiose plans, make sure you are committed to them to avoid feeling like an idiot when you quit them.

If there is no passion or excitement for your goals, don't waste your time. You might as well watch TV instead—you'll be in the same place in the end anyway. Once you have actually committed, your passion will overcome fear, laziness, self deprivation and whatever else is keeping you down. Don't be afraid. If there is something you want to accomplish, go for it full throttle and don't look back, listen to nay-sayers, or give yourself an out. And here's a gem from the pseudo-Chinese-Thinker himself: "He who burns bridges doesn't walk backwards." If you are successful, you must hold yourself to a higher standard, and maybe that's the scariest part. Lose the fear and let her rip.

Other kinds of fear that can derail you are health fears, fear of death, fear of losing your job, your spouse, your house, a Martian leaning down to grab his Starbucks and crashing his space ship into your prius. If you humans wanted to, you could worry yourselves sick twenty-four hours a day over thousands of things. Lose the fear. A healthy respect for reality and things that might go wrong is good, but living in constant fear and worry over things that may or may not happen is not good.

If you are losing sleep over your earthly fears, and can't seem to drop the fear, break the cycle somehow. Go for a walk, listen to your favorite music, bake a cake, do some push-ups, think about a happy time in your life, whatever. Procrastinate the fear and the worry or decide on a course of action and take it, but don't let your own brain eat you from the inside out by allowing it to worry. Remember, you control your thoughts, and if what you're thinking makes you uneasy, *change it.*

LAZINESS

Is it easier to think a positive thought or a negative thought? As I watch You-Know-Who try to turn me into world peace, I can't help but think that for him and probably a majority of humans, the path of least resistance in reaction to a negative or neutral event or some kind of change would be to the negative thoughts. Why? As most people slog through life at their chosen INNATE HAPPINESS, they allow themselves to be influenced by outside sources. They find themselves reacting negatively to the different things that happen in the course of their lives, rather than maintaining their preferably high INNATE HAPPINESS. It seems that with humanity, bad or negative things just sort of happen, hence the term, "stuff happens." As lame as this explanation for negative events is, it is brimming with the truth.

If every human stayed in bed all day every day, much less stuff would happen. But because you humans are always on the move, driving your machines and going through the motions of life, the laws of physics as well as nature, time, and space come together to provide an endless supply of accidents, fires, deaths, diseases and other stuff. There are reasons for all these things, but rather than rack your brains and actually waste time trying figure out why, you say, "stuff happens." And that's ok, because whether you know why they happen or not, they were and are going to happen anyway.

So if bad stuff just happens, where do good happenings come from? Here's the difference now, why your minds tend to react toward the negative. Bad news, or stuff, just happens. Good things are *made* to happen. They had to have been planned, and so when something positive happens, it is usually the result of efforts over a period of time. When the good results are in, they were half expected anyway, and do not surprise anyone, nor do they attract human interest. "That's nice", say you humans, and a bunch of you gather in your suits in a hotel ballroom somewhere and pat each other on the back.

The event may or may not make the news, but because it is a positive thing, and not surprising, it just doesn't hold human interest like a sensational, surprising, bloody murder that happens without warning. It is a sad truth that you humans are simply more interested in dirty laundry, and consider clean laundry no laundry at all. Listen to the words of Don Henley's "Dirty Laundry" song—you'll get the picture.

"No news is good news" is a statement that would perpetuate the belief that news is inherently negative, and so your society has decided that if it isn't negative, it isn't news. A shooting victim coming out of the hospital is not reported, but the shooting itself makes page one. Human nature, I guess, but if you don't give in to mental laziness, you can still be concerned yet let bad news roll off your back like water off a duck's, and not allow it to affect your HAPPINESS.

Feeling empathy for the problems of others is fine, but no matter how bad you feel about what happens to someone else, it will not lessen what happened in the least. On the contrary, too much empathy for others can actually make you sick because this self-punishment in the form of thought can break down your immune system just as worry can. If the plight of others pains you that much, don't beat yourself up about it by feeling bad, do something about it. Send money, join the Peace Corps, anything that will stop the guilt or whatever it is that is keeping you down..

Because good things don't just happen but are made to happen by you humans, and because bad news is more interesting, sensational, and surprising, it is easier for your brain to assume a negative reaction to bad or even neutral things happening. And so we arrive at negative thoughts being the path of least resistance when reacting to outside influences or changes of any kind. If left on automatic, your mind will react this way unless you maintain your INNATE HAPPINESS and you make the conscious, more difficult decision to remain positive. It is more work to stay happy and positive than it is to stay negative.

Now that you know this, when you react negatively to an outside influence, you can recognize it, and know that your mind is being "positively lazy." When it comes to maintaining your INNATE HAPPINESS and your positive mental attitude, don't be lazy or I'll transfer you to the Russian front. Schultz!

RATIONALIZATION

You humans have a remarkable mental tool that you can use to justify thoughts or actions that you know are wrong, or at least are against the principles of human law, morality and your own good. Criminals know before they steal from or kill a person that these actions are against the law, yet they do them anyway. Their rationalization process is more powerful than their sense of morality. If you have lived on this planet long enough to know what it is to cause injury to or steal from someone, then you know it is wrong. Yet there are those who do it frequently and with gusto because in some twisted way, they have rationalized that killing and stealing and abusing are ok for them to do, even though they know it is wrong.

The U.S. criminal justice system does an inadequate job of deterring crime because it is too lenient. In Saudi Arabia, if you steal, your hand is cut off. There is very little stealing in Saudi Arabia, not that Writer-Boy would want to live there. What I'm getting at is that you can, through rationalization, justify in your own mind, anything you want.

You humans are experts at using rationalization to undermine your own goals. Let's say you are thirty pounds overweight, and you want to start a diet to lose it. For about a week, everything is going great. You have avoided all the bad foods and overeating, and have worked out religiously. You have even managed to lose seven pounds and your clothing is getting looser. What could be better? How about a reward? You rationalize that a huge mound of chocolate lava cake dripping with fudge and topped with a scoop of ice cream might seem like the right thing to do. So rather than getting it and eating only a little, you eat the entire thing in one sitting.

Your friends are amazed and frankly, not surprised. Oh, you'll get back on tomorrow you exclaim, but after you finish and are stuffed like holiday sausage you get depressed because you've blown a week's work in ten minutes. You swear to yourself that the next day you'll be back on, but on the way to the office next morning, you stop for coffee and get a box of donuts for the "others", and eat seven of them in your car! You can't bring the box in half empty so you hide it under the seat and devour the rest of the donuts on the way home. You've blown two days now, and eat a huge, rich dinner. The next day you weigh yourself and are really depressed, because you weigh more now than when you started the diet. You wonder why you even bother and decide you were meant to be fat, sinking into your old routine until next time. How do I know all this? I've watched old Hunt-n-Peck go through repeated cycles as he wrote me down.

You rationalized that you deserved a treat for being good, just a couple bites, and that the immediate taste bud gratification of eating cake was more powerful than the thought of blowing your success. Even before you ordered the lava cake, you believed you could get back on the diet, but somewhere you knew you couldn't take the pressure and pain of cake deprivation, so you employed the next tool.

SELF-SABOTAGE

With this little gem, you have a perfect method for trashing the success you have already achieved and sink right back into your comfort zone, whether it be smoking, over-eating, or whatever. Let's face it, in your fat comfort zone you've dealt with being that fat before, no problem, plus you get to eat cake. Not to mention there is no pressure to maintain weight loss, or fear of failure. Another possible explanation could be that the seven pound weight loss mentioned in the previous chapter was simply enough. You worked hard, saw results, and that was it. Your lack of commitment simply allowed you to give up. So you give up and pour on the food until you reach critical mass, then start another diet.

This concept can be used to trash any goal that seems a bit too difficult to attain, such as quitting smoking, getting a raise, writing a best-seller, anything. If you attain even a small amount of success toward anything, DON"T BLOW IT! You will know when your old pal self sabotage rears its ugly head. Rather than suppress your awareness of it using rationalization, get control of yourself and work through the temptation by distracting your self with any activity that will direct you away from your vice. Get away from the smokes or donuts or by going outside or singing happy birthday, whatever it takes to avoid trashing everything you've worked for in a couple of weak seconds. That idea for a book or play or invention was once the most exciting thing you could think of. Why allow yourself to give up? Don't give up! Perseverance is 90% of all success!

ALWAYS ASSUMING THE WORST

Another thing to keep in mind when negative things happen and threaten your HAPPINESS is that often times, adversities are turned around, and what at first seemed like the end of your world, later caused it to be better than if the bad thing never happened at all. The mind is funny that way. Before assuming the worst case in a situation, wait until all the facts are in. You might just be putting yourself through a disaster that has not and will not happen. And that is needless stress and anxiety that can, as I mentioned before, make you sick.

While visiting Paris, the dude who wrote me decided to stash his wallet in the inside pocket of his jacket instead of in the back pocket of his pants. While walking through a jewelry store a man bumped into him. He thought nothing of it until several minutes later while walking down the street, his friend and he decided to get a beer at a café. Crisis-Man reached for his wallet inside his jacket and panicked. It was gone, most likely lifted by the guy in the jewelry store. Or maybe he had left it in his room, he thought. They headed back to the hotel in hopes of finding the wallet there, as our worry-stricken hero contemplated the nightmare of canceling credit cards, replacing licenses, and the possibility of identity theft. Halfway there, something made Disaster-Man grab his back pocket and hey! It was there! What a relief. A wave of HAPPINESS swept over him. The thief had actually taken the wallet from Victim-Man's jacket pocket , then returned it, intact, to his pants pocket—right.

Hey, remember Rodney King? Getting the stuff beat out of himself by the cops probably sucked while it was going on, but eventually it made him a millionaire who uttered possibly the most famous and prophetic words of the 90's: "Can't we all get along?"

Though in the wallet example, the bad thing didn't actually happen, in Writer-Wannabe's mind it had. For some reason, with Pencil-Neck anyway, when the existence of the bad situation is in question, he automatically assumes the worst. What an idiot. Maybe it's just him and maybe most of you do that, but to put yourselves through the bad situation when it hasn't been confirmed yet is, well, to put it mildly, not consistent with the size of your brain.

If you do assume the worst, and the worst is the case, then maybe you think you are better prepared to hear it. If the worst is not the case, you get that shot of relief that may bring your HAPPINESS to the level it was before. So what is better? A needless period of despair then relief that leaves you in the end, at the same level of HAPPINESS as though the situation had not occurred, or the discipline to not let yourselves experience the pain of a possible bad situation until you know it has been confirmed.

Rather than letting your survival-instinct, fear mongering brains run amuck over what might turn out to be nothing, choose not to live the problem until it is reality. I suppose if Word Smith-Boy could control his brain better, he would choose to not experience the fear until he absolutely had to. But between me and you I don't think he's that smart. Whichever way you go with the unknown, you now have a choice as to how you will deal with it. Lovely!

INTOLERANCE

No person has any more right to occupy this planet than anyone else. Though some will be more "important" in a social sense, that does not make them better, nor does it give them the right to judge others not held up artificially by fame, money, power or their own ego.

These four vices can actually take people over and make them think they actually are more important and even better than the "little ones." These most humanly desirable things have no power in the spirit world, where all truly are equal.

Some can handle these powerful attributes and employ them in the betterment of the world, while others only grow hungry for more. Hearty congratulations to those who realize that they are in a position to help the greatest number of people and do so readily and generously. Fame and fortune and power are responsibilities that only the strongest can deal with, and that's why few attain it and even less should be allowed to.

In the court of the raging media, fame, power and money give rise to royalty, while in the court of the cosmos, all humans are the same. To look down on any human as a lower form of life, no matter what their situation, is not consistent with a positive mental attitude. Intolerance or self-elevation above others is a silent negativity that most don't try to suppress and that the enlightened have risen above.

Because you are human, you are intolerant of others by nature. Overcome it and it will be one of the greatest contributors to your happiness of all. I'm not saying to simply let it be if your inconsiderate neighbors are blasting music all night—call the cops! But to hate or look down upon another human that you don't even know just because, well just because—then you are the lesser human. Hey. Be good to each other and treat everyone you meet like family because one day you will find out that they are.

NEGATIVITY

Where to begin? Ok trainee, here's where you get to do something. First open your mind to all possibilities. Drop skepticism, jadedness, and your hard candy shell. For a few seconds, blank your mind of all thoughts and feelings.

Now think of all the negative thoughts, feelings and emotions that you allow yourself to dwell on and how they hinder your HAPPINESS. Write them down. Then imagine how it would feel if you never experienced any of them again. Imagine your life without them. Feel it. No negativity at all. Let yourself experience it *right now*. For a few seconds, deny all negativity a place within you. No fear of lack, of being alone, of anything. No greed, no hate, no dissatisfaction, they are all gone. The stresses of life are completely absent, it's just you in quiet existence. Just be. Repeat this often, for as long as possible each time. It will only do you good.

EGO

Your human ego gets you into more trouble than you realize. It is your personal sense of fairness and pride and the desire not to get pushed around that begins most personal conflicts. The problem arises when the person doing the unfair pushing around, doesn't think he's doing anything wrong, or does the pushing on purpose.

For example, say human #1 is driving in the left of two southbound lanes at or above the speed limit. Human #2 comes from behind, also in the left lane but much faster. Human #1 believes he has the right to occupy the left lane, which of course, he does. Human #2 believes human #1 should get out of the way and move over, which would be both courteous and wise, but not required. So Human #2 takes offense at what he believes is Human #1's insolence, and rides #1's bumper, flashing his lights and honking, while the right lane remains completely clear!

Human #1 is offended by #2's attempt at intimidation, and not only refuses to move, but slows down, enraging the irrational #2 even more. Both drivers now are in a situation in which the first to back down is the "loser", and nobody wants to "lose." The situation escalates, one driver pulls a gun and both cars wind up out of control. Over what? Rather than referring to the ensuing crash with injuries as an "accident", Safety-First-Man calls it an incident of ego, which many "accidents" really are. Who was right? Neither. Here's another perspective for both drivers:

Let's say #1 is driving in the left lane, again at or above the speed limit. He checks his rearview and sees a car spinning out of control, approaching from directly behind at a great rate of speed. The right lane is clear, and if #1 doesn't move, he will be hit from behind. Without hesitation, #1 moves over, letting the crazily spinning vehicle by, and then slows down to see what the crazy car will do next.

Why did #1 move over in this case, and not in the first situation? Because there was no perceived intent to intimidate, and holding his ground would result in a wreck. There was simply a danger that could be avoided by moving over, and so that's what #1 did, thankful that he was able to get out of the way in time. Why couldn't #1 perceive #2's original high-speed approach from behind as a danger and move over to get out of the way, just as he did the spinning car? It's safer to have reckless drivers in front of you, so you can watch them and react when they do crash, so what's the difference? Ego. Human #1 should have moved over prior to #2 getting close enough to intimidate, if for no other reason than there was an avoidable danger approaching from behind.

Now let's say #2 is driving in the left lane at his normal, excessive rate of speed, and the slow-moving car in front of him blows a tire, and spins crazily but stays in the left lane. Without hesitation, #2 swerves into the right lane to avoid crashing into the spinning vehicle, relieved he was able to get by without crashing into it. There was an avoidable danger ahead with no perceived intent to hold ground, and #2 did what was required to avoid a wreck. Why couldn't #2 perceive #1's original slow speed in the left lane as a danger and move to the right to pass, just as he did with the spinning car? Ego. Human #2 should have moved over and slowed down slightly, well before reaching #1's position, if for no other reason than there was an avoidable danger ahead. Humans. Ha!

On a more global scale, ego gets entire countries into trouble. Let's say a giant category 5 hurricane hits the U.S., destroying several large cities and causing thousands of deaths and billions of dollars in damage. There was no human intent, and hence there can be no blame or revenge exacted. No ego involved. Stuff happens.

Now let's say a foreign country or faction blows something up in the U.S., causing thousands of deaths and billions of dollars worth of damage. The result is an invasion and an ongoing battle in which hundreds of thousands will die. Both sides think they are right, and nothing will change that. Why could the world not be deemed a "dangerous place", and the unexpected attack an unavoidable danger? Ego. Both sides think they are right, but who am I to say? One thing I can say, as long as there are humans, there will be war. Unless of course, everyone reads me and increases their HAPPINESS, turning war into a thing of the past.

If everyone could dump the ever-present importance of their ego, the world would be a happier place, with less human conflict on all scales. How can you rationalize the ditching of your egos? By letting the other guy "win." In so doing, *you* have decided the outcome of the conflict, or prevented the conflict altogether, and assumed control of the situation. In essence, you have controlled Human #2, the aggressor, by *allowing* him to pass, and not allowing him to put you in danger. What #2 has done by trying to intimidate #1 is lowly, dumb egoism. If #1 takes control and allows #2 to pass, he has taken a God-like position and prevented a conflict.

The same goes in situations where you know something is right, yet another human maintains a bogus argument. Don't stand there and argue, simply get off the subject and move on because nothing you can say will change their mind. Let them be right because they are in their own mind. There is way more satisfaction to be gained from exhibiting Godliness than there is to be gained by egoism. You humans hold the power of peace in your very minds, yet as a species you choose not to use it. If I had a head I would be shaking it right now in disgust. Luv Ya! Seeya!

PROCRASTINATION

Raising your INNATE HAPPINESS score is not hard, but you may be required to change some of your habits. For example, if you are an expert procrastinator, you will find that if you just do whatever it is you are putting off, you feel great. You feel so good that as the item approaches completion, you will think of other things to accomplish next. You might even fall into chore frenzy, in which, the more items you knock out, the more you want to do. Eventually, you will stop working and look around at all the things you can do in just a matter of minutes, many of which might have been bugging you for months. Don't procrastinate.

The one thing you should procrastinate is all worry of things that have not happened. If they do happen, once again, take action as there is no time to worry. This is not to say stick your head in the sand when a future problem is indicated. If the possibility of the bad thing won't leave you alone, fix it now. Do something, anything that moves you toward a possible solution. What I'm saying is, if it's that big a deal, take action now. If not, don't let it eat your quivering, jelly-like brain. If at any time you feel like you need to worry about a possible problem that won't immediately be confirmed, formulate a plan for dealing with it later, then PROCRASTINATE all worry. Don't waste any more brain-time on it than you already have, until all the facts are known. Twinkies. Mmmm.

LOW SELF-ESTEEM

Do you have a sneaking suspicion that you are an unloved, under paid, unattractive, misunderstood, overweight loser? Brace yourself, now. If your mind actually believes that to be true, it will make you do things that not only perpetuate that belief, but it will also make others believe it too. *IF YOU THINK YOU ARE A LOSER, YOU MIGHT JUST BE ONE.*

Now that we have that straight, here's the really cool part. Your brain doesn't care if your beliefs about yourself are positive or negative. Either way it will fulfill whatever prophesy you throw at it, simply because you believe it. If you believe you are smart, attractive, well adjusted winner, your subconscious will find ways to make it so, and your attitude will cause others to believe it too. Have you ever heard the phrase: You are what you eat? True enough, but here's the big truth: YOU ARE WHAT YOU THINK.

People tend to minimize or downplay their achievements, and sensationalize their faults. Why? Got me, I'm just a book. What I do know is, if you visualize yourself the way you want to be, believe it, and never compromise these thoughts, you will slowly become that new you. You will start doing little things that will make your visualization reality.

How do you go from the belief you are a loser to believing you're a winner? First of all, do whatever it takes to gain self-confidence. If you have to get svelte or lose weight or get another job, only you know what would give you more self-confidence. Do it! As you become more self confident, you will feel it and so will others. You will start to put standards on yourself that before didn't matter, and movement toward where you want to be will gain momentum.

One thing, though; you can't get to where you want to be if you don't know where it is. In other words, set goals and work toward them. Don't just commit to "losing weight" or "getting in shape." You must be specific, using actual numbers, dates and details pertaining to what you want.

No matter how much of an inferiority complex you have, look inside yourself and there is always something that you can do better than others. If you do have a complex, you will tend to down-play your positives. It's time now to take all the things about you that are good, and play them to the hilt. Brag about your drawings or your poems or stories, or how smart you are in math or how well you play baseball or sew, anything! If you can't make yourself brag to others, brag to yourself. In your mind, you know what it would take to dump the low self esteem. If you don't, just ask yourself what it is that the people you think are better than you have that you don't, and get it. If you are happy, you will project a positive aura that others will notice, be attracted to, and benefit from. Good luck—we're all counting on you.

CHANGE

Change. Yes, beautiful, inevitable change. Change is the only thing of which you may be certain. Why is it then, that if you humans know that people, places, everything changes, that you are so against it? The world has changed in the seconds it has taken you to read this paragraph. Babies were born, people died, a lion has taken down a kudu, a flower has blossomed, a young bird has taken its first flight. And even more has changed since you read the first line about the world changing. It is happening all the time and for the most part, there is not a thing you can do about it.

You humans are naturally resistant to change, because it heralds the unknown, and to you, the unknown is scarier than the known. Also, you humans may resist change because maybe it wasn't your idea, you might not have a say in it, and you probably had no warning. None of these things mean change is bad.

Some changes are looked upon as bad, and some as good. The difference is how you look at them even before they happen. In the next section, you will be called upon to remember that your HAPPINESS is too important to let outside forces control it. Change is a force that can easily frustrate any human without the proper mindset. You humans make knee-jerk judgment on changes even before you know of the end result, and this negativity can affect your HAPPINESS, even if the change is to your eventual benefit. Writer-Boy's employer changed the way work schedules were created, and everyone moaned about how bad it was going to be. Though a few less employees were required due to efficiencies, most of the employees have better, more flexible schedules than ever before!

So why would Joe human not give a change some time prior to proclaiming that it "sucks"? Perhaps a change in jobs or towns or people initially sounds bad, but after a while you might wind up happier than if the change never took place. So here is where all this leads to. Embrace change. Anticipate change. Lavish in changes that occur every day because you know changes are coming, you just don't know what form they will take. And when you see a change in your town or your job or your body or anything at all you can say to yourself, "Aha there is the latest change", and wonder what the next one will be. And even if a change, after it is seasoned turns out less desirable to you, you have looked upon in the best possible positive light, and you have not allowed it to affect your HAPPINESS.

And so in order to not let inevitable change cause you frustration and uneasiness, try making it into a game. Since you know things and times and people change, you can predict even this second that something, good or bad, whether it affects you or not, will change tomorrow, next week, next year, even ten years from now. When you see a change, because you made your prediction in the last sentence, you can take credit for knowing it was coming, even though you didn't know specifics, and proclaim to yourself, "There it is!" rather than saying to yourself, "Oh no"!

Can you imagine how boring your life and your planet would be if everything and everyone stayed the same? Writer-Boy would be a greasy, slobbering Neanderthal scraping these words onto a cave wall with a rock, charging the rest of you grunting troglodytes a rat pelt and a handful of fish guts to read em, only you wouldn't be able to read, so you would just point and grunt excitedly, and because these cave shapes were new, you would realize that your world was changing and that the change was exciting and therefore, good. See? I tried to write a for-instance about lack of change, and change took place anyway. It's unstoppable!

And one day far in the future there will be a Thought-Boy who will project his positive thoughts of change directly into the brains of his "readers" and he will use Writer-Boy's computer-pecking fingers as the example of how archaic the world would still be without that inevitable, beautiful, eternal change. Embrace it, love it, expect it, because like it or not, here it comes. Guaranteed.

GET OVER IT

This chapter is strictly for those of you who blame your current unhappiness on other people, your past, whatever. Everyone else, feel free to skip this one.

The unhappiness you may be feeling right now is not your fault, because until you got a hold of me, there was no one to tell you what you are about to read. Let's assume you are a victim of whatever devil you blame for your lack of HAPPINESS or success or whatever. And let's say that the absolute worst thing happened to you, such as mental or physical abuse by either strangers or loved ones, and worse yet, at a young age. Anyway, let's say it happened last year or twenty years ago or whenever, and since then, let's assume that you somehow escaped the situation, because why would you hang around for that kind of treatment?

Yes, you are a victim of your past. They were out to get you, and they did. Because of what they did, you might never be happy again. Your background is keeping you down. Your father or your mother made you this way. Some kid made fun of your braces in the seventh grade and now you are miserably scarred for life.

Being just a book, it's hard for me to understand how some of those things can hurt you for life, but let us now assume that they have. Get ready, we are about to break open the eggshell of a new beginning, but first I will acknowledge your status as a victim. Yes, the things they did and said were meant to inflict pain on you and it worked. There was nothing you could do about it, you were defenseless. And so you have kept these wretched memories alive to the point of influencing your HAPPINESS. Forgive them, whoever they are, right now, for everything. Forgive yourself right now, for everything. None of it matters anymore. Let it go.

If the past or whatever is still keeping you down, you have either lost control of your thoughts, or are allowing your past to control you because you want it to, you've got some kind of attachment to it, or you just don't care. Past treatment by others is not your fault, but if these horrible things are still influencing your HAPPINESS, well, as of now, that *is* your fault.

Up to now, your past may have negatively influenced your HAPPINESS and it's not your fault. That's the last time you'll read that from me. You, and only you, now that we have established that, are obligated to fix it. You know about the past, and if you think the past is still keeping you down, I'm here to tell you, get over it because it has gotten over you. Keep the sweet memories, ditch the ugly ones, and move on. Do you want fries with that?

PART III.

21 SECRETS TO HAPPINESS

We've already laid the ground work for increasing your overall HAPPINESS. Again, your INNATE HAPPINESS is chosen and maintained by internal decisions, whereas your HAPPINESS is more easily influenced by outside forces. Our goal is to increase your natural tendency to be happy, and lessen the extent to which you allow outside forces to lower your HAPPINESS. From the first section of me, you may have figured out your INNATE HAPPINESS number. Is it still the same number? Decide what your number is now. This will be the baseline from which you will track your future INNATE HAPPINESS as well as your HAPPINESS at any given time.

The following 21 chapters (secrets) will raise both your INNATE HAPPINESS and HAPPINESS. Since both states are so incredibly inter-dependent, many of the following subjects will apply to both.

1. SET HAPPINESS GOALS

Now that you have decided what your INNATE HAPPINESS is, Where do you want it to be, and by when? Let's say you think your INNATE HAPPINESS is a 2. What would you like it to be? Think about that for a moment. Remember, the scale goes from -10 to +10. If you could change your INNATE HAPPINESS simply by saying one word or thinking one thought, what would your desired INNATE HAPPINESS be? Ok, time's up. If you said you want to be a 10, congratulations, you win.

Some suit from Writer-Boy's legal team decided that there is a portion of you humans that might read the next paragraph and cause yourselves harm, then try to sue Writer-Boy for something YOU did. So put on a snorkel, because you're going for a dip if you didn't say + 10 to the previous question. It's kind of like the woman who sued McDonald's after SHE spilled hot coffee on herself. Such frivolous lawsuits have absolutely nothing to do with justice, and everything to do with an opportunist trying to use a legal system run amuck to make themselves rich. It would be like Writer-Boy suing every person on the planet who didn't buy this book, for causing him mental pain and suffering, as well as financial hardship, in addition to feeling shunned by society…Excuse me, I've got to have Writer-Boy make some calls.

I'm back, sorry for the little legal tirade, but you tort-happy humans forced me into it, there was no choice. Ok, back to HAPPINESS goal setting. If your goal is to have an INNATE HAPPINESS of ten, you are correct! If you chose a number less than + 10, put on your snorkel, dip your head in the cool waters of your nearest toilet, and flush once for every point less than +10, patiently waiting for the happy tank to refill prior to each successive flush. (hence the snorkel). For example, if you desire your INNATE HAPPINESS to be a 7, that'll be three flushes or if you said 5, then five flushes please. Now!

Did you do it? Did you give yourself the prescribed swirlies as Ape-Man has told me to order you to? I hope you said no, because if you flushed your head down the toilet because I told you to, you're in worse shape than I thought. Good thing you had a snorkel on.

In way more words than necessary, why would you want to be any less happy than the happiest you can possibly be? You want your INNATE HAPPINESS and your HAPPINESS to both register a 10 every day, all day for the rest of your life. Is that possible? Hard to say, but if you constantly strive for the max, you'll know that whatever numbers you get will be as high as they can possibly be.

How long will it take to raise your INNATE HAPPINESS to where you want it? That's up to you. Writer Boy, even though he is writing me, still gets frustrated at other drivers when they do unexpected and dangerous things. One method he has used successfully to not let other drivers drive his HAPPINESS down is, expecting them to do the dangerous things before they do them. When in the vicinity of other vehicles, he thinks about what each driver might do to cause an accident, and mentally runs his reaction through his mind. If the other driver does a stupid thing that was anticipated by our boy, he revels in his ability to predict the future as opposed to getting wound up at the person. It's just a way to look at what makes you crazy a little differently, so those things don't make you crazy and bring down your HAPPINESS.

Any outburst of anger, be it aloud or in thought is stress that detracts from your INNATE HAPPINESS, your HAPPINESS, and even your health. Getting back to how long it will take you to get happy, it's entirely up to you. Just remember that once you reach your desired INNATE HAPPINESS, you'll have to work to maintain it through a positive outlook.

Now that we have discussed setting HAPPINESS goals, it's time to set your life goals. What are they? Hey, I'm just a book. You got the spongy, quivering, pudding-like brain. Ok, I'll tell you my goals. As a book, it's my goal to get as many clones of me made in as many languages as possible, so that I can achieve world peace, and—relieve you of some of your filthy money. Two services for the price of one. Are you happy yet?

It is also my goal that I affect everyone who reads me in a positive way, no matter how small. If all a reader gets is a chuckle, that's good enough. If I help only *one* of you humans to be happier for one second of your life, I have won. What's the best possible situation for this book? To help every current and future human to live happier Earth-lives, resulting in world peace. Even better would be for every human that reads me to help other humans to live happier lives using what they learn in my pages, again resulting in world peace. If you read even one thing that helps you get happier than you were, spread it around, eh? Oh, one more thing—I want at least one copy of me around as long as you humans exist.

Ok, now that I got that off my cover, back to your goals. Is there anything you want to do, to be, to see, to have, anything. Do you want to fly to the moon, or end armed conflict, or meet Nick Cage? How about just losing a few pounds or doubling your income? What do you want from the rest of your life? Do you just want to be happy or do you want to make everyone happy? This is where you can dream of whatever you can think of that you want to do with your remaining time. Some of these things may not be possible, but that doesn't mean you can't imagine what attaining them would be like. Try it. What would you do if you were the richest person on the planet? Just imagine what it would be like, what you would do with your money and time. Ok, you can't live all these dreams, but you can imagine them.

Try this—As you drift off to sleep every night, think of what would make you the happiest right then. As you fulfill your life-long dreams in your mind, the residual HAPPINESS that lingers from the thoughts alone will boost your INNATE HAPPINESS. You might even get to dream about your goals, and let's face it, when you dream during sleep, your dreams are dream reality. Whatever happens in those dreams is real to your dream consciousness.

"Seeing" these life long dreams come true in your mind's eye will cause you, even in the smallest way, to live those dreams as though they were real. Try it. Sappy? Absolutely, but here's a question—So what? Oh, I know, people will think you're sappy, and make fun of you. Ah-huh. First of all, you don't have to tell anyone about how sappy you are, and second of all, if you care that much about what other people think of you,…don't.

Some of your way-out dreams may actually be within reach. If they are, go for them however you have to, to include what I have just described. What have I just described? Visualization, of course. Writer-Boy has used it many times to get what he wanted, including a job he wanted all his life. He also used it to get published, job promotions, many things. You can use it too. How does it work? You imagine a situation as though it is really happening. You put yourself inside the goal, feel the textures, see the things playing out just like you want them to, and make it as real as possible. Your brain really doesn't care that these visualizations have not happened yet. It will produce the same positive thoughts because it can't tell the difference between a dream, reality, and a visualization.

If you make yourself believe that you will reach that goal, your mind will arrange for you to do the things that could make it so. You are what you think, as I mentioned in an earlier chapter. So however impossible your dreams are to attain in the physical world, anything is possible in the visualization world. Make the neuron connections through creative visualization and those connections will be recorded in space and time, and might just become reality.

Set your HAPPINESS and life goals and visualize them. Don't forget to visualize those that are physically impossible too. Oh, one more tidbit about goals. How the heck can you get what you want if you don't know what it is? Ta-ta.

2. LOWER YOUR STANDARDS

Yes. To be a happier person, you must make it easier to recognize a happy event. In other words, if you need to win the lotto in order to be happy, it's likely you never will be. But if you lower your standards, so to speak, or you allow little things that before meant nothing, to contribute to your HAPPINESS score, your level of HAPPINESS will rise. The more little things you notice as good, the more likely the sum of them will increase your overall HAPPINESS, whereas before, achieving the same level of HAPPINESS used to require a significant event.

It may sound a little corny, but you're going to have to recognize something as simple as making a green traffic light a great thing. It means you save time, wear on your brakes, and the fuel required to accelerate after a red light. If you can think of more, do it. It's all just a matter of looking at things a little differently. If in the beginning you feel like you are having to lie to yourself to find the good or the joy in something mundane, then lie away.

Eventually your mind will generate these good thoughts automatically. When that happens, voila! You will be a happier person.

Something as simple as waking up well-rested should be noted and enjoyed by thinking about all the good things that come from a great night's sleep. Some people take that a step further and celebrate that they've woken up at all. Or maybe your favorite song comes on the radio. Enjoy your good fortune and bask in the feeling the song gives you.

If you can take positive things that before you barely noticed and make them into a good happening, you will spend more of your time thinking good thoughts. This, coupled with your downplaying of negative forces, thoughts and events, will make you a happier person much quicker than just accentuating the positive or downplaying the negative without doing the other.

At the same time you lower your standards for what you consider a positive event, you must raise your standards or threshold, if you will, for what you consider worthy of making you feel angry, frustrated, sad, worried, threatened, hatred, or any other negative emotion. Use the powerful negative thought neutralizing questions. Remember:

What is good about this?

How can I turn this situation into something positive?

What can I learn from this?

Is it really *that* important?

These questions are mainly for outside threats to your HAPPINESS, and are one way to deal with them. We also have our positive thinking which raises both your INNATE HAPPINESS and your HAPPINESS. If you have raised your INNATE HAPPINESS, and you use these questions to neutralize negative thoughts or events, the negatives will exert less influence on you than before you started reading me. Are you starting to get the picture that you really

do have control over how happy you are? Thoughts control HAPPINESS.
You can control your thoughts. You control your HAPPINESS.

Try this: When any little thing happens to go your way, say or think
these words: "Things continue to go my way." The more you say it, the more
things will go your way. It works for Writer-Boy, and it will work for you.
Even if things sometimes don't go your way, say it anyway, knowing a goody is
just around the corner. He swears this ONE LINE will change your life for the
better as it has done for him. Take a ride on the Reading.

3. TAKE CARE OF YOUR VEHICLE

Would you put gas in your car that you knew would help to wear it out sooner than normal? Would you force more gas into your car's gas tank than it can hold? Would you let your car sit idle in the garage for months at a time without even starting it? Then why would you do it to your body? Fat-Boy can't talk, but I can. A little less soda and chips and a little more water and fruits and vegetables. A little less TV and a little more exercise, even if it's just walking. You can buy a new car, but your body is the only Earth vehicle you've got. When it's gone it's gone. Next time you find yourself treating your car better than your body… you know, I don't feel like getting into it with you right now. Do what you want, but you'll pay for it sooner or later. You know exactly what I'm talking about, Pilgrim.

4. MAINTAIN A POSITIVE OUTLOOK

A POSITVE OUTLOOK stands for positive mental attitude, or that which is indeed the key to HAPPINESS. You must greedily pursue HAPPINESS like some pursue money. When you make a capital gain in HAPPINESS, make it only whet your appetite for more, just as money does for some. But how much HAPPINESS is enough? The same question can be asked of money. You can never have too much HAPPINESS, nor can you give too much. It is not greedy to want to be happy, but in alignment with your purpose. Never stop your quest for more and never forget that by following my instructions and by simply denying negativity and appreciating the many positives available, that you can have as much HAPPINESS as you want. Remember, you are as happy as you want to be. When you do get a dose of HAPPINESS, let your personality spread it around.

As for money, it seems that when you don't have it you grope for it, and when you've got it, you're afraid you're going to lose it so you grope for more. So how much money is enough? That is for each to decide. This little comparison does not mean you can't be rich and happy, nor is it meant to infer that less money means more HAPPINESS. What it does imply is that if you are going to obsess over something, make it HAPPINESS.

Ok, back to A POSITVE OUTLOOK. You can have a positive outlook or a negative outlook. Which one you want is for you to decide. What it means, according to Sunshine-Boy is that every thing you think has a positive spin to it. In essence, you become your own spin-doctor. When Ernest Shackleton's ship broke up in the Antarctic ice pack over 800 miles from the nearest human, his positive attitude was enough to get him to civilization, then sail back and rescue the rest of the crew. Without Shackleton's POSITVE OUTLOOK, the entire crew would have surely succumbed to the elements. *Endurance*, says Adventure-Boy is a heck of a read, and might put a new perspective on your all-too-modern everyday problems.

It would seem that every human who has braved and beat insurmountable odds, could not have done so without A POSITVE OUTLOOK. Call it optimism, a POSITVE OUTLOOK, whatever you want, great things just don't get done without it. If Edison had a negative attitude he could never have completed the thousands of experiments required to invent the electric light. Do you think Donald Trump loses sleep at night over the bankruptcy of one of his casinos? No way! He knows that failure is but a stepping stone to greater successes, and that if you succeed 6 times out of 10, you are a success.

Look at everything with a more positive view than you have before, and you will help to boost your INNATE HAPPINESS. GET A POSITVE OUTLOOK!

Here's what Writer-Boy calls The PADRA Principle, use it! Maintain a POSITIVE attitude. ABOLISH negativity. DEFINE your positives and good things in your life. RECOGNIZE a positive when it comes your way. APPRECIATE your positives. When negativity attacks, think PADRA!

5. WORK OUT, EAT RIGHT

Writer-Boy is no one to talk about eating right and working out. He works out at a local gym maybe three times a month, and is on a perpetual diet, maintaining his physique at about 30 lbs. over-weight. He has found though, that when he is looking trim, he feels his best. Then drinking soda and eating chips become more important than feeling good (imagine that). When it all comes down to it, you've got to do what feels right for you. If you don't drink soda, and you eat broccoli every day, good for you. In Cake-Boy's case, he drops some weight, declares good enough, then proceeds to chow and drink soda again. Then he sees himself one day in the mirror (mostly by accident) and says, "oh my God, what a slob!", and then jumps back onto another diet.

Since Keg-Belly obviously has no idea how to be healthy, I'll give you a few pointers. First of all, don't overeat. Work out five times a week for at least twenty minutes (anything that breaks a sweat). For each meal, eat no more than the prescribed amount from each food group. Four to six ounces of lean protein, ½ cup of high-fiber grains or a couple slices of whole grain bread, unlimited fresh vegetables (no, mashed potatoes loaded with butter and cream are not unlimited. Think man!), and 1 piece or 1/2 cup of fresh fruit.

Don't eat fried food, snacks from a bag, or sweets except maybe once a week. If you do eat sweets or snacks, make it the good stuff. No fat free, sugar free crap (unless you're diabetic). Just eat your cheesecake or whatever and be done with it (this will keep you from feeling deprived and downing a whole wedding cake later on). Don't eat between meals. Drink lots of water. Heeeey, this is starting to sound like... MODERATION! No, it's the Tuff Luv diet. There you have it. How to be healthy in A couple paragraphs.

By the way, though in Svelte Wannabe's opinion it helps, you certainly don't have to work out or eat healthy in order to be happy. Nor do you have to be thin. But Writer-Boy has come to refer to working out as a "happy pill", and it is truly the easiest, quickest way to boost your happiness without ingesting something. No, you don't have to run a 10K, just go walking.

WB finds that listening to music on his mp3 while walking helps him to go faster by walking in time with the tunes—slower for the slow songs, faster for the up tempo songs. After about 30 minutes, the music and the motion become addictive and you find yourself setting mini-goals that usually get updated. WB will have gone 45 minutes and burned 320 calories, but he notes that 400 calories is not far off—so he keeps going. Then he may switch to a goal of one hour at the 51 minute point Hey, before starting this or any diet or exercise program, consult your physician. Sound official enough?

If you think the Tuff Luv diet is junk, just remember that weight gain or loss is only a matter of math. If you take in more energy than you burn, you'll get fat. If you take in less energy than you burn, you'll lose weight. Any questions?

Here's a little gem about "wasting" food. If the food is on your plate, you are not wasting it if you are full and don't eat it, even if you throw it away.

It will not help a starving person elsewhere in the world to have food if you clean your plate. It will only make you uncomfortable, fat, and unhealthy. As a matter of fact, it is more of a waste to eat food you don't want than to throw it out, because you are wasting your body. For those of you still plagued by the "Clean your plate" mentality, and you can't make yourself throw unwanted food away, PUT IT IN THE FRIDGE! If world starvation really bothers you, box the food up and take it to those who are starving, or give money to those who might feed the hungry. These actions would actually help the starving. Eating an over-sized blob of mashed potatoes and gravy after you are already full will not. Nor will making an already full child clean his plate. On the contrary, it will only perpetuate the "clean your plate" mentality that has no doubt helped to make the U.S. the fattest country on the planet. Nicely Done!

P.S. Repeat these axioms when your will power fades: "Losing weight is easy and fun, and feels better than anything tastes." "Fresh fruits, whole grains, fresh vegetables, and lean meats." "Working out, even something as short as a ten minute walk, is the quickest, healthiest happy pill there is." See you at the gym.

6. STOP, DROP and ROLL

This is what your friendly neighborhood fireman will tell you to do if you find yourself in the unfortunate event that you are on fire. Well, we are also going to use the phrase to put out mental fires that cause worry, depression, uneasiness, self-sabotage, dissatisfaction, sorrow, temptation, and any other condition that might threaten your HAPPINESS. We will specifically use it as a cycle-breaker in that when you feel an unhappy, angry, or sad feeling or a self-destructive action approaching, you can think of these words to stop the cycle of negativity. CAUTION: STOP, DROP and ROLL is a MENTAL EXERCISE! If you forget and actually do it, make sure to wear a helmet.

As an example, if you are in the process of kicking any undesirable habit and find yourself tempted to blow it, mentally STOP, DROP and ROLL to keep yourself from going off it. Before you put that donut or pill or cigarette or whatever in your mouth, think of the words and break the cycle, then put the item down, back away from the item, and do something else. Leave the room or do some push-ups or drink some water, anything to get away from the temporary pleasure of the bad thing, and the permanent displeasure of maintaining a disgusting, harmful habit.

We'll use the eating of a donut as an example for how to avoid temptation. It takes about one or two minutes to eat a donut of say, 300 calories, and roughly 40 minutes of walking at 4 miles per hour to burn 300 calories. Immediately following the mental STOP, DROP and ROLL (from now on abbreviated by SDR), and changing your thoughts and actions to anything but the donut, you will project yourself three minutes into the future and imagine having just eaten the donut and all that is left is a greasy film on the roof of your mouth and acidic grease-burps from your protesting stomach. The pleasure of the donut at that point will be gone, but the damage it will do to your body and hence your HAPPINESS will linger for perhaps years!

Once you have avoided the donut for the amount of time it would have taken to eat it, you will feel no different by not eating it than you would feel if you had eaten it because it's pleasurable effects would by that time be gone, and what would remain would be the disappointment of blowing your health program, and the knowledge that you are running the donut through your veins via your blood, and in effect, running the donut through your heart itself! Now there's a thought. Would you grind up that donut in a blender and have a doctor inject it straight into your heart? No? Well that's exactly what you are doing when you eat one, all for about two minutes of taste bud pleasure. Sobering, isn't it?

You can use the SDR method for any thought or behavior you want to avoid. The grind-it-up-and-inject-it-into-your-heart method can be used for any undesirable substance that you feel you can't do without, even though you know it will cause you harm, and that the damage to your body, unless you control it, will be cumulative. Finally, consider that the act of consuming the undesirable food or substance could take a measurable amount of time off your life, hence, eating that donut is now a life and death decision. In the next chapter, life and death situations are described as being of utmost importance. Are you prepared to make a life and death decision while standing over a box of donuts?

Remember, to avert an impending food or substance violation of your body,

1. SDR
2. Project into the future. Will the long lasting after affects be worth the temporary pleasure?
3. How will you feel after the pleasure is gone?
4. Would You Inject it Into Your Heart?
5. Is it worth the time it will take off your life?

This stuff can work with any vice that possesses you, not just unhealthy eating. You can use this method for smoking, drinking, and even addictions that aren't ingested, such as gambling. When one of you humans is successful at changing unwanted habits, you might attribute the change to a "program" of some type, or a drug or something else that aided you. If you did indeed make the change, it was all you, baby, because you wanted to. Don't give the credit to the means because the means can't decide to change and take the action for you. You do it yourself.

7. IT'S *HOW* IMPORTANT?

Negative and positive events happen throughout your human lives. Some just happen, while some are brought on by you. How you choose to look at them will determine their affect on you, and consequently, how they effect your HAPPINESS.

As an outside observer, I see you humans as not knowing what level of importance you should assign to daily events, and in many cases, you allow positives to go unacknowledged, and minor negatives to be assigned an improperly high level of importance.

A friend of Nervous-Man once backed his car into a tree. Nervous-Man asked the friend if he was mad at himself, to which the friend replied, "No, it's just a car." So the friend had assigned a much lower level of importance to the event while Oh-My-God-Man thought the appropriate response was to scream and worry about insurance and slam the steering wheel with both hands. This caused Oh-My-God-Man to ponder his friend's reaction and think about how great it was. There was no screaming or worry or anything. The friend simply drove off and eventually got the car fixed without a second thought.

Another time, Mr. Impatience and the same friend were waiting for a train to pass, so they could keep driving. Old Short-Fuse started complaining, while the friend looked at the situation as an opportunity, got out of the car and laid down in the lush, green grass in the median and watched the clouds go by. Short-Fuse eventually followed suit, and found himself hoping the train-delay would last longer!

Both of these examples showcase the proper way to assign importance to minor events over which you have no control, and the second example shows how you can turn a minor negative into a positive by simply changing the way you think about it. The path of least resistance with you humans is almost always to the negative, while a lucky few have the gift of turning such minor problems into a neutral or even a positive event.

There is no physical labor or study required to be able to think about problems in a positive way, it's just a matter of controlling your thoughts. If you find yourself reacting negatively to something minor, use the cycle breaker--STOP, DROP and ROLL. You don't actually have to do it (unless of course you are engulfed in flames), just use it to change your thoughts. The result will be a happier you.

Most of you humans can handle the big things that happen in your lives because you are human and resilient, and even more so because you have no choice. Your spouse wrecks the car, and you rise to the occasion by remaining calm and focusing your concern on the people, not the car. As I watch Lap-Top Man and the humans around him, it would seem that the large events, though life-changing, are usually dealt with more appropriately than the little things. It would seem then, that the small inconveniences and daily setbacks actually affect your INNATE HAPPINESS and HAPPINESS more than the big things, simply because you don't know how to assign the proper level of importance to the little things, and because more small things happen on a daily basis.

The big things are a no-brainer, and so mentally, there is absolutely no confusion as to how important they are. You either accept them and deal with them or you wind up in a fetal position next to an overflowing dumpster in some dark downtown alley. So if the reaction to a big, highly important negative event is calmer than that of say, getting cut off in traffic, why do you humans freak out in a road-rage moment when that guy cuts you off? Well, what do you have to say to that?

If you remain calm for large events, why can't you do the same for little things? Let's say your young son or daughter accidentally knocks your sewing machine off the table or accidentally tips over your Harley. Most of you humans would launch a tirade at the child that would leave them wanting to run away. If, ten minutes after these minor accidents that you felt required a scream-fest, your child was abducted, you wouldn't think twice about dropping every dime you own to get your son or daughter back. So why yell at them in the first place? Because you don't know how important the event is.

You are assigning these minor things global importance when they don't deserve it, and you need to stop it because it affects your INNATE HAPPINESS. There are certainly better ways to show disapproval to *anyone* than to raise your voice or resort to the unspeakable, heinous, cliff of physical violence.

Here is a simple method with which you can more accurately assign importance to any event that would lower your INNATE HAPPINESS or HAPPINESS. Again, we will be assigning importance on a scale from zero to ten. As you can see, if the problem is not a life and death event, it is simply no problem at all. It may take some time, but these problems other than life or death will eventually be resolved. Let go of your pride, your money, your possessions if you have to, they will never be as important as your life or the life of a loved-one. I guess what eats you humans up is the fact you can't resolve some relatively minor problems NOW. And you can't stand that unresolved problem hanging in limbo. Hey, when something pops up, give yourself six months to fix it, and if you fix it sooner, there's even more cause to be happy.

0000000000000000000000000000-10

No Problem   Life and Death

As No-Problem-Mon mentioned earlier, you humans can usually handle the big things, and it's the little things that make you blow up, so he will leave the big stuff to you, and you can use the scale to determine the importance of anything relatively minor before you react, as the little things seem to drive you humans bonkers.

Again, let's say your kid tips over your Harley but he's not hurt. Look at the scale and determine where the event falls on the scale. If it's not a life and death situation, it's no problem, and that's what you should consider it. Just say to yourself, "No problem." Fix the scratched exhaust and go on with your life. Before blowing your stack for any reason, ask yourself if it is a life and death situation. If it's not, don't assign it a higher level than it's worth. If it helps, you can use the stuff happens rationale. Take away the kid's video games or whatever, but just remember, screaming is mental violence, and harmful to both parties.

If you assign every little thing that happens in life an importance score of ten, you will drive yourself and everyone around you nuts. Remember, when something is upsetting you, the first step is to mentally STOP, DROP and ROLL. Then project your problem onto the importance scale and decide which of the two categories fits it the best. Either way, take the appropriate action and move on. The point is, if your problem is not a life and death situation, don't treat it like one.

On the other hand, positive events that raise your HAPPINESS and INNATE HAPPINESS should be milked for every second of positive thought you possibly can. Dwell on these positive thoughts and if the event pertains to someone else, congratulate them profusely and help them milk the situation to their greatest benefit. Always be happy for the success of another human. It's a boy!

8. TWO WORDS TO SET YOU FREE

Most man-made industrial systems that involve air or liquid under pressure are protected by a means to relieve over-pressure situations. The normal method is to place a pressure relief valve in the system that releases excess pressure at a point lower than would damage the system. Your home's electrical system also has the same type of protection in it's built-in circuit breakers that trip for various electrical faults. Why all the tech-talk? Because I am about to bestow a pressure relief valve or circuit breaker (your choice) on your often overloaded brain.

From the last chapter we learned that the most important events or problems in your human lives should be life and death situations. With respect to global absolutes, everything other than life and death events can be classified as No Problem. If you think your job or your money or toys are equally important as your life or the lives of your loved ones, you have a warped sense of values. For example, let's say you've fallen overboard while on a Caribbean cruise. It's night time, and you have no life vest. Would you not give up everything you own to be rescued? Heck yes! That's life and death.

When your brain is getting overloaded by the obligations and pressures of everyday life as a human and you just can't take one more bit of bad news or negativity, free yourself by employing two little words. Can you guess what they are? I introduced you to them in the last chapter. Drum roll please…NO PROBLEM! Just say it ALOUD, repeating as necessary, until you realize that these situations that are causing you to lose sleep, or worse yet the will to live, are not life and death, and therefore not worthy of the harm they are doing you.

Once your mind has cleared and you realize that problems at work or school or losing 50 grand in the stock market don't even come close to life and death seriousness, you can reset your circuit breaker and get back to doing whatever it is that you humans do in your lives. Hey, if you want to make up your own pressure-relief phrase, jump on it. For instance, say to yourself "I don't care" or "It just doesn't matter." It's entirely up to you.

Another test you can give to your situation to measure its importance is the death-bed test. When you are laying there with maybe a week or even a minute to live, will you be glad that you worried about something that was eventually resolved? Everything is eventually resolved. What if the amount of worry you spent on a subject took a month off your life? That would be hard to measure, but wouldn't you be disgusted with yourself if it were true?

So Super-Dad-Wannabe's son has been bugging him for months about being taken to a paintball course, and yesterday they piled into the car and left. Ten minutes after leaving, the son announces that he forgot his equipment. Normally, Dictator-Man would have jerked on the brakes, whipped the car around, and sped off toward home quite upset. But since the event occurred as Calm-Boy wrote this chapter on importance, he calmly turned the car around, remembered there was something that he forgot too, and returned home with only one editorial comment.

He had asked himself the questions and found there was something good about the return home. The situation had actually proven the usefulness of the importance scale. The first thing he did was to mentally Stop, Drop, and Roll. Then he put the setback to the importance test. He found that his son's forgetfulness was not a life and death situation and said to himself "No problem, I forgot something too." Believe it or not, he felt better because he had put his son at ease by not ripping into him and trying (I can't believe you humans do this to each other) to make the poor kid feel like an idiot. It worked! The importance test method of diffusing a frustrating situation had actually worked with Writer-Boy, which means it could work for anyone! Dogs too!

9. SLOW DOWN

It seems you humans have an uncanny ability to be strictly results-oriented and to dismiss process as an incredible burden. You've got to have things NOW, you've got to get there NOW, and anything that delays your plans of blissful immediacy turn you into a raving lunatic. So you whip in and out of traffic, trying to get three car-lengths ahead like a strung-out junkie looking for his next fix, putting every other car in your path in danger, all so you can get there thirty seconds sooner. You know who you are, and this one's for you.

Or your flight is delayed due to weather, and you feel the need to rectify the situation by ripping into the gate agent with the same voracity you might use if someone had just set your house on fire. Is this you? If so, why? Please list in your mind all the reasons for driving in a way so as to endanger others, and for berating another human for a problem over which they have no control. Let me help. Now say it with me. "Because I have no control over my mind or my actions when my expectations are not met, and consequently some innocent person should be endangered or berated in return." Please imagine the people in the other cars as your family members and the gate agent as your spouse, your child, your parent, your best friend. Would you still do it?

How can we fix this automatic outrage over every situation that doesn't go as planned? Slow down and consider the journey as part of the adventure and equally as important as arriving at the destination. Get control over your mind, knowing that this internal rage you feel over minor delays is hazardous to your health as well as powerless to make things happen any quicker. It has no merit, and hence, no reason for being. You can also lower your expectations. Sure, make your plans, but the lower your expectations, the easier it will be for you to handle unplanned delays and things that come up.

Slow down. As much as you may hate drive-time and wait-time, you might as well not waste it being mad. Free yourself from the insidious pressure of having to get there faster and enjoy the ride. While waiting for anything, listen to some music or people-watch or remember some good times or laugh at your favorite joke or read the paper. Whatever you do, don't write the time off as wasted when you could use it to make yourself happier. If whatever you are doing or wherever you are going is not worth the time that must be spent traveling or waiting, don't go. You gotta be somewhere, and whether you are stuck in traffic or standing in a long line, you most likely put yourself there by choice. If it is worth the time and effort, know that the destination would not be possible or even as enjoyable without the journey, and that heavy traffic is a chance you take every time you turn the key.

Today, Writer-Boy was driving home from a road trip on the two-lane highway leading to his home after the Memorial Day weekend. Careful-Man was driving about seventy-five feet behind the car in front of him, ten miles an hour over the speed limit. A white pick-up truck came roaring up from behind, riding Writer-Boy's rear bumper. When the pick-up finally passed, the driver laid on his horn and cut violently back into Writer-Boy's lane, narrowly missing

Calm-Man's front bumper. There were plenty of cars in front of Writer-Man before Impatient-Man passed, so he wasn't really getting ahead anyway.

By the time both cars reached the toll plaza, Impatient-Man was stopped in front of our hero, the rear bumper of the pick-up about three feet in front of Writer-Boy's car. What was gained by Pick-up Man? Nothing. Pick-up man probably knew he wouldn't get anywhere quicker, he just wanted to pass Writer-Boy because there was too big a gap in front of Writer-Boy, so I-Own-The-Road-Man felt the need to put everyone in danger for really nothing.

Most traffic accidents are caused by someone doing something stupid. Humans may not intend to cause a wreck, but their impatience causes their vision of reality to be in conflict with reality itself, causing the wreck. Be careful out there, and stay off the phone. All skate!

10. SPIRITUALITY

According to God-Like wannabe, you don't have to be spiritual to be religious, and you don't have to be religious to be spiritual. The notion that you humans retain a spirit that continues on after you leave the planet can be comforting, and help to alleviate the fear of your eventual demise. Religious doctrine attempts to explain how and why your spirit is preserved and where it eventually winds up after the big fall. It also tries to shape your actions in the mean time.

Many turn to religion and prayer in bad times and they find that it helps them survive. Belonging to a group also is an important part of this comfort for many. If you find that belonging to a certain group helps you, by all means, do it. Same goes for those that don't believe in a higher power. Whatever makes you happy.

One question to those who think there is no spirit or life after death: Since you will be gone after you die, are you living every second of your short existence to its fullest? Another question to the devout worshipers of (your God here): Because you will be saved and living with (your God here) after you die, are you living as happily as you possibly can, and the way (your God here) says you should? Would you try to live fuller if somehow you found out there was no afterlife?

The previous questions were not meant to be answered, but to provoke thoughts on just where your life is, based on two opposite philosophies, neither of which have ever been proven. They are neither meant to shake your faith nor bring you to religion, but to assess where you are versus where your religion, or lack thereof, says you should be.

If going to church helps you to be a better human and also alleviates your fears and makes you feel good, by all means, do it. But if your religion is keeping you down or less happy than you might otherwise be, what are you doing? Or if your religion is telling you that you should kill yourself or someone else (you know who you are), perhaps you should ask for clarification from your church leaders as to exactly how your untimely death is a better choice than a happy life, and why they have not made the same choice that they demand of you. After they answer this question (the answer will be inadequate), you can find out their real views on death by saying, "You go first." Their response should help you to form an intelligent, logical decision, that is if you are not too far gone.

Wouldn't it be just human luck for there to be an afterlife if you believed in it and none if you didn't believe? Hey, don't look at me, I'm just a book and I'll be around as long as there's a Library of Congress. Cheerio!

11. BE CREATIVE

There are few things in life that are more satisfying than the act of creating something. It doesn't matter if it's writing, making a dress, building a garage, or making a cake. There is no one on the planet that would not benefit from the satisfaction of creating. Sure, it helps to have an interest in your subject. How about making a Mother's Day card for your mom? Or building a doll house for your daughter? Write the great American novel or make up a funny song or build a bird feeder. The very act of making something where before there was nothing is one of the HAPPIEST things you can do. It doesn't have to be a big deal, just *something*.

If you claim to not have a creative bone in your body, try creating a smile on someone else. Get some kind of kit that provides everything you need to make a…poodle—I don't know, all I know is that Writer-Boy has derived a huge amount of Happiness from writing, cooking, building drawers and cabinets, models, recording his own music, home improvement projects, even just planning a day and getting everything done that needed to be. Paint your bedroom or get a new shower curtain. Repair something that needs it, or make it better. Half the things you humans do requires creativity but you don't realize it. How about this—try doing your job the best you've ever done, with the quality that you complain about not being around any more. Just for one day.

Here's an idea. Take your job or your hobby, something you know about and enjoy, and build a website that gives the information away, while at the same time making you money by putting ads on your pages. Writer-Boy is doing that with me at www.happiness-quotes.com. He's not giving away the store, and he hasn't made a dime, but he's having a blast. Check out Site Build It, who showed WB how to build a site from scratch.

12. LIVE FOR TODAY, PLAN FOR TOMORROW

It would truly be fun to blow every dime you make on cars, trips and toys. But even squirrels bank nuts for the winter. According to most TV financial planners, most married couples should have cash on hand equivalent to three to six month's salary for emergencies. These talking heads also say workers should "max out" IRA's, 401k's and any other retirement accounts available to you. There is a happy balance for each of you humans, and only you know what that is. Starving-Writer-Boy has always tried to live well below his means, carrying zero credit card debt, living in a small house, driving an eight year old car, and get this—using his big brother's old stereo speakers circa 1973! But if he feels like dropping a couple hundred bucks on a weekend getaway on occasion, he does it without batting an eye.

If your bills are higher than your salary, you are screwing up just like your government. The only difference is that they can print more money at will. If overdue bills and calls from collection agencies don't bother you, let her rip, man. But if you are losing sleep over your finances, it's time to contact Writer-Boy's Debt Consolidators. Just kidding. You must determine your tolerance for debt and your capacity for making the payments before you go buying large-ticket items on time.

You can save all your money for retirement or spend it as quickly as you get it, but a happy medium can be struck, along with some sort of savings plan that can fit any income bracket. If you don't have the discipline to live within your means, get help. Find your balance between income, bills, saving, and expenses, and stay within your means. Just remember that overlooking the present while preparing for someday could be cheating you out of valuable happiness by focusing on someday instead of now. You own the now, and someday may never come so don't forget to live for the day. Dude!

13. DO SOMETHING FOR SOMEONE

There will be opportunities for you humans to do favors for each other by exerting very little effort. Be on the lookout for these situations and don't hesitate to help someone if you can.

Several years back, Captain-Man was fishing on his boat, when another boat that had run out of gas flagged him down. So Samaritan-Man called the Coast Guard and also called a towing service, then remained in the area, waiting for the tow-boat to arrive, as the other boat had no phone or radio. After more than an hour, and convinced the tow-boat had screwed up the GPS position, Rescue-Man threw the stranded boat a line and towed the boat until he was able to get the rescue-boat turned in the right direction, and finally in sight.

The purpose of this story is not to showcase how great a guy Writer-Man is, but that day his afternoon of fishing was pretty much ruined by screwing around with these people who lacked the common sense to determine how much gas they had when they left the dock and to carry a working radio or cell phone. At first he was perturbed that he should take time out to ensure the safety of the people aboard the stranded boat and then to have to tow them for an hour, but after the tow-boat showed up and he was back to fishing, he felt a satisfaction that would not have emerged without having helped the distressed boaters. What started out as a royal pain turned into that which made the day because Mother-Theresa-Man may well have saved the people's lives, or at the very least, a long, lonely night on the Gulf Stream.

You certainly don't have to save a life to get the unique satisfaction one gets from helping someone. Hold the door for someone or let another car merge in front of you or just smile. It doesn't have to be big. You may not recognize it, but when you give to others without expecting anything in return, a wave of Happiness will course through you that cannot be gotten any other way. It doesn't have to be a stranger either. Help your spouse in ways that you normally don't. Call your favorite aunt just to talk. There are so many easy things you can do to spread happiness that to not do them is only denying yourself the personal HAPPINESS you could reap from them.

So do something for someone and expect nothing in return. It's a good thing. Martha rules.

14. LIVE EVERY DAY LIKE IT'S YOUR LAST

If you have never lived as though today might be your last day, try it. Yes, we are only talking about a way of thinking, but I hate to break the news to you that you have no guarantee that you will wake up tomorrow. What if a Martian driving by in his ship leans down to grab his cup of Starbuck's and crashes into your house, cooking you to a crispy critter? Laptop-Man is trying to make light of the idea there are no guarantees on how long you'll be around, but let's face it—there are no guarantees.

The guy who wrote me once thought he might have one of those life limiting diseases. While he waited a month to find out, his mind considered all possibilities, and decided that no matter what, from then on, he would find the joy in everything; from the sound of the wind in the trees to the sparkle of the sun on the waves. From the joy of an unsolicited hug from his son to a passing peck from his wife. Why couldn't he have thought that way before his little scare? And why don't all of you think that way with or without a scare? I know, because you think you will live forever, right? Anyway, here's the rest of the story.

So with one foot in the mental grave, my creator vowed that nothing would rattle him or make him mad, because as far as he was concerned, he was quite possibly a goner. So for that month he was happy a good part of the time, in between hourly waves of panic, but he had actually found more things to be happier about. For example, his son got a snap together model of a T-Rex skeleton with a kid's meal. So Old Doomsday decided to put it together, and accidentally put the legs in the arm sockets and the arms in the leg sockets. I don't know if it was stress or what, but that little screw-up provided him with a good ten minutes of hysterical, gut wrenching, eye-watering, fall-on-the-floor laughter as he pondered the visual before him.

I wasn't around back then but I'm sure I would have been proud. Either that or I'd have hurled myself at the back of his head. Would he have laughed that hard or even at all before? He had found the joy in everything that he could, but later, after the pure joy and HAPPINESS of a clean bill of health faded, he found himself once again getting caught up in the din of life, cussing at other drivers and moping when little things didn't go as planned.

And now, years later, he found that his life had faded to a 0 to 1 on the HAPPINESS scale. Perhaps his subconscious saw this and made him write me as much for him as for you, dear, duck-breathed reader. That doesn't matter though, what matters is that he recognized he had the power to make himself happy, and that the power must be exercised like a muscle in order to keep it strong.

Models on T.V. with ripped bodies don't get to that point and then quit working out because they finally made it. They have to keep on working out or they will lose it much quicker than they achieved it. HAPPINESS is not something that happens to you, it's an attitude that must be constantly monitored and exercised lest you wake up one day and it's gone. I'm not saying that there aren't people who are naturally very happy, because I'm sure there are. But I'm willing to bet these lucky ones are the exception, and the rest of you are the rule.

To realize that your time is limited just might cause you to do things for yourself and others that you might not otherwise do. What would you do right now if someone told you that you had the rest of this day and after that, nothing.

You can't count on actuarial tables or assumptions to figure out how much time you have left. Last week a teenager was killed by a drunk driver who drove her pickup right into his bedroom as he slept at 3 A.M. The only thing you can count on, the only thing you really ever own is this second. Everything else is gravy, so treat it like gravy. Achtung!

15. LIGHTEN UP!

Hey, like the chapter line says, lighten up. Don't be so serious, duck-breath. Sorry, I had to. When the joke's on you, don't get mad or even, laugh, even if you feel you've been dissed. Laughing is the opposite of stress. Every second you spend in laughter will help you to live longer, plus, laughter might just be the epitome of HAPPINESS itself. Every time you get one of those gut-wrenching, fall-on-the-floor, laugh-so-hard-you-cry moments, this might just be as good as it gets. Make it last as long as possible, and think of the reason often. Take every opportunity to laugh, even if you don't find the joke particularly funny.

If you take yourself too seriously, it is easier to feel as though you've been disrespected, and resort to anger and irrational outbursts. Things bother you more than they should. People will want to avoid you because of all that seriousness. To take yourself seriously is to expect too much from life, from other people. It is a vice of the ego. Extremely important jobs can be done with unspoken seriousness and a light-hearted demeanor. One question you can ask yourself in order to bring seriousness or worry into perspective: Will this still be a big deal next week, six months from now, ten years from now?

Being serious is a form of worry, so being serious about non-life-and-death situations may be putting undue stress on yourself. Yes, there are things that are better taken seriously, like the quality you put into the job you do, but this isn't about that. This isn't about you being serious about things you think require it. It is about being serious about you. And that is a function of ego.

Can you laugh at yourself along with others? Or does that make you feel hurt, and want to get revenge? Maybe your mental skin is too thin and you let things bother you more than they should. You are the most important person in the world to you, which means you are not the most important person to anyone else. They have their own problems to deal with.

Where is all this going? The less serious you are about everything, the better. Writer-Boy is the picture of overkill when it comes to being somewhere on time. But he keeps that seriousness in the background and prevents stress by leaving early, knowing full well he'll get there on time. Since he gives himself more than enough time to get there, time is not a factor and so the underlying seriousness of timeliness never surfaces.

Writer-Boy was sitting on a plane talking to an older man in the seat next to him. The subject of seriousness and vanity came up and the man said, "When I was twenty, I cared what people thought of me. When I was forty, I didn't care what people thought of me. Now that I'm sixty, I know that people don't think about me at all.." To bask in self-importance among others is to not know how the world works. Try humility. It is a true sign that you have expanded beyond the self.

16. TREAT YOURSELF

Do something for you once in a while. Get a massage or pedicure or an ice cream, or—you guessed it, a twinkie. Do whatever would really trip your trigger, that you won't normally spring for. Go get a nice meal or see a movie or buy a book or go fishing in Alaska. Whatever it is, as long it is within your means and within reason just do it. You will never regret doing something like this for yourself. Can't think of anything? Treat someone else. Take your wife or husband on a trip, or send your brother on his dream vacation.

If you are wealthy and can part with some of your money without causing yourself hardship, don't just let it pile up, spread it around. Let's say you've always wanted a Rolls Royce but didn't want to dent your estate. Think about how your heirs are going to blow that money like it was nothing, and buy yourself the car!

Where was I? Oh yeah, treat yourself because there is no one on the planet that cares more about you and your HAPPINESS than you. So worrying about not spending your child's inheritance is a bunch of hooey! They'll be alright without it, and if there are siblings or step-situations from other marriages, it will only be the cause of division, greed, and disharmony among them. So spend that dough and have a ball before you're too old to do it, or worse, that Martian accidentally drives his spaceship through your noodle.

This concept applies to all of you, not just rich guys. You know what makes you happy, and once in a while you've got to do something for you. It doesn't make you a great mother to buy your kids all the newest toys and not drop a dime on yourself. You are worth it, so drop some dough on you.

By the way, treating yourself does not always have to involve spending money. Take a hot bath, or head to the coast to watch a sunrise. Hide for an afternoon and read that novel that's been sitting around since Christmas. Do something for you, you'll be glad you did. I'll be back.

17. APPRECIATE WHAT YOU'VE GOT

Why not? It's you who have created the ownership of your current life situation, including your house, car, spouse, kids, toys, money, or even the lack of any of those. How can you appreciate that run-down little house of yours that you are absolutely sick of living in? Don't look at what it is, look at what it very well might be after a tornado, an earthquake, a fire, a hurricane, or a Martian crashing his spaceship through it. Your creaky little hovel is far better as is, in one piece, than a multi-million dollar mansion trashed by a mudslide. And people, rich and poor, lose houses they are sick of every day and wish to God they had them back just the way yours still is. Hard to say no problem after losing your house, but if you are still alive, you must appreciate *that* because of what might have happened to you while you were in your house as it was being trashed.

Hate your job? Imagine your boss walking up to you tomorrow with a cop and a box full of your stuff out of your desk or locker and saying, "You don't work here anymore, here is your final check, you need to leave." Would you still hate your job and thank your boss for the best day of your life? Or would you feel kind of bad? If you hate your job that much, look for a new one while you are still working, then quit once you find one. But if you aren't actively looking for a new job and aren't thinking about quitting, maybe you should quit complaining and try to enjoy your work instead of perpetuating needless negativity.

Can't stand your spouse? Imagine waking up tomorrow and looking out your window to see your him or her getting into a limo with some other him or her. Forever.

Ever think your life might be easier without your kid because he or she drives you nuts? Some of you humans obviously do, because every few months some whacked-out mother kills hers.

If you ever feel this way, for whatever reason, imagine them gone, never to be seen again. It seems that kids cause the most stress when they are living at home, and maybe sometimes you look forward to an empty nest. Do ya ever? Well one day those candy-eatin', Nick-watchin', bike ridn' little pukers are going to be house guests in your house and right about then you'll be wishing that they were the same age they are *now*. Project yourself into the future and imagine yourself almost begging your sons or daughters to come home for a visit which might happen once or twice a year if you're lucky. Why is it that you humans don't appreciate (like the song says) what you've got till it's gone? Well, from now on, when you start getting sick of what you've got, remember to appreciate it BEFORE it's gone.

Here's a new one. Learn to appreciate the things you lack. "What? Are you nuts? "How can I appreciate the lack of any of those", you say. Well you can. If you have more money you have more to lose. No house? No roof damage or blown out screens or taxes or insurance to worry about. No, you won't get an investment out of renting, but when the central air goes out, you call the landlord and forget about it as opposed to dropping $8000 on a new unit. Let's face it—like the other song says, freedom's just another word for nothing left to lose.

Don't complain about the lack that you have created for yourself, take joy that you are free of being a slave to a house, a car, a bank account, whatever it is that you think you want but don't have. Yes, you can appreciate the simplicity that not having things allows. Let's say, just for fun that you win a Ferrari in a contest. At that point you are a "kept person." Yes you are kept by the desire to keep that car looking brand spanking new. If someone bashes their door into your old Chevy, no problem. If they do the same to that new Ferrari, your world comes crashing down. It's just a car. If your world revolves around a toy, you might be better off without it anyway.

And when you hit it big and finally have all the stuff you thought you wanted, enjoy them, but remember, life and HAPPINESS are not about toys, or money, or stuff…it's the people. Once you get the toys, you will tend not to appreciate them long. Appreciate what you've got—first the people, then your money and your stuff, as Suzy Orman says . And don't forget to appreciate the simplicity provided by what you don't have. You'll be much happier.

One more thing—This chapter is not about dropping goals or killing dreams or ambition. It's about how you think as you chase that next dream. It's not about giving up or declaring "good enough" when you have dreams yet to realize. It's just about looking around when you wake up and knowing that what you see is a reflection of the reality you have created for yourself. Yes, you humans always want more, bigger, better, and there's nothing wrong with that.

Remember that perseverance is the mother of all success, but as you persevere, enjoy your surroundings, your stuff, especially the people. Human life hangs by a proverbial thread every second of its existence, and can be snuffed at any time. Enjoy the people around you and tell them often how you feel about them, lest one day you go looking for a psychic to do it for you.

18. GET A LIFE

In other words, get a reason to live, other than that you happen to still be alive. Whether it be a hobby or children or grandchildren, business or sports, traveling, music, charity or playing tidally-winks, passionately pursue your cause because you love doing it. What? There is nothing on Earth that you could possibly be passionate about? This might require you to dig into your memory and shuffle through all the things you wanted to do in life but never did. Pick one and go for it. Find your passion and live it. YES, YOU CAN. Now you say it, "YES, I CAN"! It's never too early or too late.

19. ENJOY

You humans think in words. Whatever thought your brain happens to create at any given time is sent to your language center for translation into your own everyday speech. If you have a positive mental attitude, your words will reflect that and force you brain to use positive words in your thoughts whenever possible. Words with the prefix en are often associated with positive emotions or actions. Enlivened is but one of the many words that demonstrate this point. Enlivened may be described as giving cause to liveliness. The crowd was enlivened when the band appeared out of the smoky explosion on the stage. What I'm getting at here is that the band *made* or *caused* the crowd to get lively. The band did not allow the crowd to get lively, in a sense it *forced* the crowd into liveliness.

Now let us examine the word enjoy. If you really love baloney, you might say that you really enjoyed the last baloney sandwich you ate.

If you agree with the premise of the last paragraph, *you* caused or forced yourself to feel joy or to be joyful because of the baloney sandwich. " I enjoyed the last baloney sandwich I ate ", means you forced the joy on yourself, due to the good feelings you associate with baloney. Though the baloney is surely the catalyst, it did not force the joy, you did. Did you enjoy your last vacation? If yes, you might say you forced joy on yourself due to your last vacation. Surely something had to have gone wrong, though. Lost luggage or a delayed flight, bugs in your hotel room, bad weather, whatever. In spite of whatever little setbacks you encountered on your vacation, you still caused yourself to be joyful and to have fun *because* you were on vacation.

If you can force joy on yourself during your vacation, even with all the minor setbacks, what would stop you from enjoying life, simply because you are alive? "Oh, that's different", you might say. Well, if you use the analogy that you are a spirit vacationing on Earth, and you enjoy vacationing despite any unforeseen setbacks, then nothing at all should keep you from forcing joy on yourself during your Earth-vacation, your life. If you don't buy that, why don't you humans force joy on yourselves simply because *you can?*

Try this—for a five minute period, think in *feelings only.* Don't allow words to shape what's going on in your head, because they are man-made, and there is much more to this world and you than man-made anything.

Since you humans do have the ability to force joy on yourselves, why wouldn't you enjoy every second of every hour of every day because joy is a good feeling and you want to feel good? Enjoy your life, and your life will be filled with joy. It's your decision. If your hard candy shell prevents you from taking joy in your own creation and continued existence on Earth, then you must learn to…

20. FIND THE JOY

In everything. Yes, you can. But in order to avail the beauty and wonder of your world and the universe to yourself, you must drop the workaday boredom and jadedness and cynicism that keep so many of you down. Under your tough, hard candy shell is the very same thought machine you possessed as a child. In a sense, no matter what your age, you are still that child and always will be. Oh, sure, your bodies change and you become older and you look in the mirror and wish you were young again, but it doesn't help, and you must learn to accept that your vehicle, just like a car, deteriorates with age. And rather than bemoan your body's old age, you should celebrate it because you have been allowed to experience so much on your field trip to Earth.

I hope Writer-Boy can practice what he preaches when the time comes, but just because you are eighty or ninety doesn't mean you can't think goofy, funny thoughts or tell jokes or even watch cartoons. Apparently, your society has decided that you humans must act a certain way based on the age of your vehicle, when it is entirely possible that you are not your vehicle at all. Perhaps you are the very same spirit you were before you arrived on Earth, and the only difference between then and now is that your vehicle is getting closer to being worn out. You are not your body. You are a spirit driving your body. If you allow your society to restrict your thoughts and actions to that commensurate with the age of your body, then you are missing out on a whole lot of joy that might otherwise be available to you.

I know, it's easy for Middle-Aged-Man to say all this because he's only 45 and hopes to live long and prosper. Perhaps he can come back in thirty or forty years and read what he wrote and maybe it will help him to find joy as his vehicle nears the end of its usefulness.

Back to finding the joy in everything. I think where Philosophy-Man was headed before he went off on a tangent was that since you spirits never really change with the age of your bodies, where does the child-like wonder and curiosity and excitement go? It doesn't go anywhere. It's still there, but you living as the body's age have squashed it with the quest for love and HAPPINESS and financial security, doing all the things that bodies of your age do.

When you begin your lives, your worlds are made up of toys and dolls and cartoons and curiosity. Then you concentrate on BB guns, makeup, and that apparatus "down there." Then you move on to the opposite sex, with a sprinkling of life-ambition in some. Then you decide on a direction for your life, whether it be specific or a blank calendar, and marriage, cars, paychecks, taxes and diapers enter the picture. And with the diapers come the flashbacks of your childhood, and your views of yourself as a child don't change because you are still the same, you just know more about the world and are now responsible for another life. So you progress to the 401K, refinance, college fund stage and now you have a little empire, and in addition to the responsibility to that young life, you now have something to lose in your little nest egg.

And so you lose the simplicity of your life and are chained to cell pones and market indices and ball practice and low carb and one day you wake up and you wonder where the time has gone and realize that it's almost over. Worries over Social Security and pensions and Medicare and wills take over and you realize that retirement is not the sleeping-in, free for all, not a care in the world, panacea you thought it would be.

And through it all, the you that has no age waited to be let out but was suppressed and will be until your time is about up, then you will let it out, but it will be too late to bring joy to the "blurry years." I'm not trying to rain on your parade here, I'm trying to get you to see how much happier you can be if you just let yourselves. Your body's age has nothing to do with your HAPPINESS.

It has been a long road, and now that Writer-Boy has described but a few of the reasons for you to find the joy in the here and now, here is how. It is so simple that it may seem insignificant, but here goes. Drop your defenses, your ego. Return to innocence. Release the ageless you. Lose the time-hardened meaning you have assigned to events, people, circumstances, and view your "problems" from afar, as an outsider, knowing that in time, *everything gets resolved, everything comes to a conclusion that is ultimately for the better, and things are the way they are right now because that's the way they're supposed to be.*

Force yourself to think of all you have to be thankful for, even if you've become so blinded to the positives in your life that only negativity shines through. Focus on the good in your life, and the things you want—not on the things you don't want. Drop the jadedness, cynicism, and emotional defenses you have built over time and know that you are a good person, and because you are good, you like, even love yourself for who you are. Know that others cannot possibly know you with the depth that you do, and may not see the good in you with the clarity that you do.

When you love yourself for the good person you are, you will no longer feel the need to prove *anything* to *anyone*. You will stop defining yourself based on other people's opinions. How can they possibly know you completely? They cannot, and for you to resent their negative opinions of you is to allow them to control your happiness. When you are completely comfortable with who you are, self-esteem is automatic. This is not ego inflation, but self-love to the point that the ego, and defense mechanisms are no longer required. The truth in you is profound love and self-respect, and these things need no defense.

With self-respect comes humility. Humility in the eyes of the cynical and jaded will be taken as a sign of weakness. To prop themselves up, the ego-driven will attack this perceived weakness simply because it is an easy target. Any remaining ego in you will want to be hurt by these attacks, but self-love, if it is strong enough, will simply see them as egocentric posturing maneuvers and disregard them. There will even be times that you inadvertently do stupid things like Writer Boy sometimes does, and the self-esteem will keep you from feeling stupid. You'll have yourself a chuckle and move on.

And with this dropping of your ego, (the same one that created your hard candy shell), you will find that little things don't bother you like they once did, and neither do the words and actions of others. It will be easier to enjoy a moment, and notice the beauty that surrounds you that before went unnoticed. If you are unsure of exactly how, try the following suggestions and then come up with your own.

Look up in wonder at the night sky and try to grasp the distances. You can't. The Andromeda Galaxy, visible to the naked eye, is 2.5 million light years away. One light year is roughly six trillion miles. Whoa. Look at a fish in an aquarium and wonder if the wild, yet symmetrical color scheme was an accident, or was it actually planned by something or someone. Continue the thought to who might have decided on the very existence of you.

Marvel at sunrise and sunset and the ever-changing sky smeared with wildly shaped, yet right-looking clouds. Smile at strangers just to see how many smile back. Listen to the radio and let songs from your past bring the feelings of those times to the now, and lavish in those happy thoughts for a while. Know that one day you will look back on your life as it is now and remember it happily.

Watch a tear-jerker movie, alone late at night and don't try to hold back the tears. Pour yourself a glass of ice-water knowing that there are people alive *right now* who could not imagine such luxury. Give a homeless person the handful of change weighing down your purse or pocket. Everywhere you look there is joy and beauty and wonder to be found, and all you have to do is open your mind to it and it will appear. Appreciate that you can see, feel, love, that you are alive. Find the joy all the time, especially when you are feeling even the slightest negativity; but don't stop there—when you are feeling really good, you can heighten those feelings by helping others to find the joy, the love, the beauty that surrounds humanity and waits to be noticed and appreciated.

Maintain your positive outlook and know that all things happen for reason, even if they hold nothing more than a hidden lesson. It's been said that when you are ready to learn, the teacher will appear, and know that this teacher can take on any form, be it a human, a personal triumph, profound joy, illness or even great loss. Though a life of ease seems most desirable, the greatest lessons are learned through adversity. Greatness is never the product of ease.

Deal with adversities without emotion, without asking why or claiming unfairness, punishment or conspiracy, and solutions will come much easier. If a situation is beyond your control, let it go. Look at the possible outcomes with curiosity, not fear, knowing that you can handle whatever comes of it. Say it: "I can handle *anything.*" Repeat it often, believe it, and you will experience more joy than you ever thought possible. That's a guarantee.

Find the joy in everything, and consider positive, the things that you used to look on with neutrality. Find the joy in everything, and consider neutral the things you used to look on with negativity. Find the joy and it will find you.

21. HAPPINESS IS A CHOICE

It's not the occurrences that happen in your life that control your HAPPINESS, it's what you associate them to, or what you think about them. The ability to associate any cause with a positive or neutral effect is within you now, just as it always has been. As you have learned, the easiest, and in many, the automatic path to their associations is the path of negativity. Choose to avoid this path and help others who don't know that they can.

Work at HAPPINESS and it will be yours, as something that desirable does not seek you out, nor does it come automatically, not for most anyway. PURVEYOR-OF-HAPPINESS himself has not achieved automatic positive associations. He must keep himself working at it, just as you must. Do it long enough and it *will become automatic*. How long will it take? It will take only as long you want it to take.

Remember, you control your thoughts. Your thoughts control your HAPPINESS. You control your HAPPINESS. Whether you take control of your HAPPINESS or leave it to circumstance, you now have the means to be as happy as you want to be. Look outside yourself to find HAPPINESS, and that HAPPINESS will be fleeting; go within and choose HAPPINESS and that HAPPINESS will never wane. Do both and you will have found the greatest treasure of all. It's all up to you now.

I'm (the book) done

Live happy

SEEya,

Writer-Boy says "Hey."

www.ingramcontent.com/pod-product-compliance
Lightning Source LLC
Chambersburg PA
CBHW030109070426

42448CB00036B/562